Reclaiming Hospitality

Reclaiming Hospitality

A Church's Guide to Hospitality Houses for Immigrants

TIFFANI COX HARRIS

CASCADE *Books* • Eugene, Oregon

RECLAIMING HOSPITALITY
A Church's Guide to Hospitality Houses for Immigrants

Cascade Books
An Imprint of Wipf and Stock Publishers
199 W. 8th Ave., Suite 3
Eugene, OR 97401

www.wipfandstock.com

PAPERBACK ISBN: 979-8-3852-5617-4
HARDCOVER ISBN: 979-8-3852-5618-1
EBOOK ISBN: 979-8-3852-5619-8

Cataloguing-in-Publication data:

Names: Harris, Tiffani Cox, author.

Title: Reclaiming hospitality : a church's guide to hospitality houses for immigrants / Tiffani Cox Harris.

Description: Eugene, OR : Cascade Books, 2026 | Includes bibliographical references.

Identifiers: ISBN 979-8-3852-5617-4 (paperback) | ISBN 979-8-3852-5618-1 (hardcover) | ISBN 979-8-3852-5619-8 (ebook)

Subjects: LCSH: Hospitality—Religious aspects—Christianity. | Emigration and immigration—Religious aspects—Christianity. | Church work with immigrants—United States.

Classification: BV4647.H67 .H24 2026 (paperback) | BV4647.H67 (ebook)

03/26/26

This book is dedicated to my husband Brent, a true partner, and to our children Hannah and son-in-law Benjamin, Emma, and Andrew who have been an unyielding source of inspiration and strength and also to the people of God at DaySpring Baptist Church for their courageous hospitality, grace, and mercy.

Contents

Preface ix

Acknowledgments xi

1 Companioning and Accompaniment 1

Companioning as Christ Companions Us 7

2 Equipping the Leader 30

Pastoral and Theological Preparation For Leaders 31

3 Equipping the Congregation 49

Educational Preparation for the Local Church 50

4 The Nuts and Bolts of Developing a Ministry 62

Vocation and Calling 63

Framing and Setting the Structure 73

The Process 74

5 Maintaining a Ministry and Thriving 89

6 Bearing Witness: A Theological and Pastoral Reflection 105

Appendix I: Questions for Reflection 115

Appendix II: Resources: Choruses, Prayers, Litanies 119

Resources 126

Bibliography 127

Preface

In an era of mass migration, the church today finds itself caught between the polarizing forces of protectionism and isolation, and the call of the Gospel of Jesus Christ, to care for the least of these in our society. Christians often find themselves struggling to know what to believe and how to understand and apply the call of Scripture to care for the stranger, the foreigner, or the immigrant. In the midst of national policy changes and heated rhetoric about immigration, I fear some in the Christian community have decided that caring for the immigrant is not a fundamental expression of the Christian faith. Caring for the outsider, the foreigner, the refugee and asylum seeker, in the eyes of some, is seen as fringe—something only radicals do. The church has become divided and angry, just like our culture, regarding how to respond to the current political and societal divisions exposed in our North American context around the issue of immigration. Immigration-rights activist and theologian Alexia Salvatierra suggests that the church is standing on "sacred ground" at this current intersection of faith and culture and that all conversations about immigration, for Christians, must begin with our Christian faith as informed by Scripture.[1]

It is time for the church to reclaim biblical hospitality to the outsider as a central component of what it means to follow Christ in ministry with the least of these as found in Matthew 25. This book, in part, seeks to provide a foundation for understanding the Christian call to ministry with those who are poor and suffering, specifically with the asylum seeker. It is a resource and formation guide for congregations and individuals sensing a call from God to extend themselves in hospitality. The project provides a foundation of Christian history and Scripture that speaks to the call of Christ to deny oneself and follow him in ministry with the least of these—those who are

1. Montañez and Estrada Carrasquillo, *Church and Migration*, 11.

hungry, thirsty, poor, and forgotten by society. Included is guidance on how to structure a ministry of hospitality with asylum seekers, essential questions to consider, and a reflection upon leadership challenges in this type of ministry. It tells the story of one congregation's approach to developing a ministry of a hospitality house for asylum-seekers and why churches should recover the discipline of hospitality with immigrants.

Acknowledgments

IT HAS BEEN A joy and privilege to recount the beautiful work of the Holy Spirit around me through the process of accompanying our new friends seeking asylum in this country. This is our story, not my story. I give thanks for the many brave asylum seekers who have shared their stories and thus encouraged and challenged us. I want to thank those who patiently read this manuscript and offered so much insight: Sarah Musser, Abby Villagrana, Cintia Aguilar, John Hunt, Deidre LaNoue, Joy Alexander, and Jennifer Davis. Your insight has been invaluable and has propelled me forward.

I

Companioning and Accompaniment

"When you cross the border, no one will be there to help you." These words uttered by a woman in Mexico weighed heavy on Maria's heart as she nervously waited in line to see a Customs and Border Protection officer on the southern United States border. Maria lived in hiding for a year in her own Central American country after the cartel pushed her family off their land. She did not want to flee her homeland but felt she had no choice. She and her other children watched at gunpoint as her husband and son were murdered. These terrorists took over her farm to produce drugs. Forever changed by the violence, they fled in the middle of the night for their safety, never to return. Seeking refuge elsewhere in their home country, the tentacles of organized crime reached far and wide and found them. One by one, the cartel hunted down their extended family and pushed them off their land and out of the country. The government was impotent to stop them.

Maria's pastor, who led a small Baptist church in the middle of this Indigenous community, continued to pray for her, and encouraged her over the phone. Indigenous persons are being pushed off their lands all over the Americas,[1] and she had papers documenting it, which she presented to the Customs and Border Protection agent at the border. The agent determined she had a credible threat and let Maria and her three children enter the country and apply for asylum. Over the course of a year, they had walked and traveled over 2,000 miles to get to the border. After crossing the border,

1. For more information, see Villegas and Robles, "Conflicts Over Indigenous Land" and Mukpo, "Nicaragua Failing to Protect."

Maria and her children walked the streets of West Brownsville, Texas, wondering and praying what they should do next. A woman from North Carolina who had been serving with a Spanish-speaking Baptist church's shelter found Maria and her children on the street. She took them to the church and began to care for them, helping them find food and clothing, a shower, and a place to rest. Over the course of a few days, Maria noted that this woman was like a mother to her, caring for her family. It was then that the associate pastor of the church in West Brownsville called me.

Our church had been praying and preparing to open a hospitality house for asylum seekers, a journey that had begun several years earlier. We were finally as ready as we would ever be to welcome our first family. With guidance from a Cooperative Baptist Fellowship missionary in the Rio Grande Valley of Texas, we met pastors and churches on the border who run short-term shelters, hoping they would refer families to us. Part of the church's discernment process led us to be focused, starting small, seeking to create space to build relationships and companionship. Rather than operating a short-term shelter with different people coming in and out each week, the church discerned its calling to build relationships with the least of the least, whom we determined, for us, was the Latina asylum seeker and her children, focusing on those who had nowhere else to turn for help. We decided to provide mid-term length shelter/housing for these women until they received their Employment Authorization Documents (EAD), which typically takes 9–12 months.

As Naomi in Scripture opened her heart to Ruth and brought her under her wing, so to speak, we wanted to create space for this kind of mutuality and hospitality. The story of Ruth and Naomi is one of reciprocity, for Naomi allowed Ruth to accompany her, taking her back to her people and her home. Conversely, Ruth also accompanied and cared for Naomi, demonstrating the reciprocity of a God-centered community.

With this in mind, church members drove eight hours to the border to pick up this exhausted family and bring them to our hospitality house. Upon arriving in our shelter, which we called "Naomi House," the mother of this family immediately called her Baptist pastor in Central America. It was a proud moment for me, as a Baptist pastor who has often been frustrated with the denomination, to see this family cared for by three distinctly different Baptist congregations along the way; it also brought great comfort to the Central American pastor back home to hear of the care these churches provided.

This story of Maria and her family and the story of how our church came to the place of accompanying asylum seekers is the background of this book. For years, I have heard from more conservative and evangelical denominations that concern for the poor and those on the margins of life was more of a liberal political ideology than a Bible-centered priority. The attitude of many evangelicals is that social justice has left Jesus behind and has become an end, in and of itself, suggesting that social justice is dangerously undermining biblical authority.[2]

I once spoke with a Baptist pastor in London, England, who was charged with the task of local mission support, who explained that social ministry that does not overtly share the Gospel by not offering the "true bread that is life" is deficient and essentially leads others astray. On the other hand, many in social ministries recoil against requiring hungry, homeless people to listen to a sermon before they can be fed. To some, this type of forced evangelism feels coerced and does not respect the dignity of those receiving support and help. While some critique ministry as described in this book as neglecting to offer the true bread that sustains life, that messages of spiritual salvation should be of primary importance before any other type of interaction and ministry, caring for the poor and the stranger can and should attend to the physical, social, and spiritual needs of those caught in the immigration crisis of our time. In building relationships this way, we share Christ's love where actions speak louder than words. Words about the love and transformation that life in Christ offers are important, yet impotent without demonstrated relationship-building and companionship.

Today's political landscape is constant upheaval and change, which is felt most pronounced with immigration. Christians are left wondering how they can respond both individually and corporately. Some are confused by political messages, while others have decided that ministry with immigrants is not essential. This book, in part, seeks to provide a foundation for understanding the Christian call to ministry with those who are poor and suffering, specifically with the asylum seeker, as a way of reclaiming the biblical discipline of hospitality. I hope it will also be a guide for those sensing a call from God to extend themselves in this way and that it may

2. For more on this ongoing debate, see https://statementonsocialjustice.com; Joseph, "One More Word"; Erickson, "Social Justice"; Roach, "Southern Baptists' Social Justice"; Sandlin, "Primer on Cultural Marxism," 10; Tennies, "Book Review: Fault Lines." Williams, "Putting First Things First."

even be an avenue through which the Holy Spirit extends an invitation to serve our asylum-seeking neighbors.

This book is born out of my church's experience as we came to share our lives with those seeking asylum. It is one church's story that might also serve as both an invitation and a guide for other churches wanting to develop similar types of ministries. It is deeply specific and personal. Our church's context, experience, and desires are unique, yet I believe that our experience can be instructive and helpful. It is a compelling story that I have the privilege to share with you. It is our (congregation's) desire that we demystify the challenge and invite others along on the journey of serving Christ specifically with those seeking asylum, and, more generally, with those caught in the immigration challenges of our era.

Eight hours from the border, deep in the heart of the red state of Texas, in a mid-sized city, our ideologically diverse church opened a hospitality house for asylum seekers, one of only a handful in the state. We knew we had so much to learn, so we started small, built a coalition, listened, reflected, and humbly began. Many often ask how a church like ours began ministry with those seeking asylum. The impetus was a humanitarian crisis at our southern border in 2018 and 2019. We heard the pleas for help from sister congregations in Texas and prayed about how we might help. The contemplative practices that have formed the foundation of our congregation had trained us to listen to the guidance of the Holy Spirit. Thankfully, the congregation was attentive to the gentle nudging of God's Spirit at work around us.

As our church began to open ourselves to how God might be calling us to minister, Pastor John Garland at the San Antonio Mennonite Church became our friend and served as a prophet to us. When the immigration crisis[3] reached an intensity on the Texas border during the beginning of the first Trump administration, our church heard the calls for help from San Antonio Mennonite Church and countless other churches along the border who were seeking to minister to the felt needs of broken and hurting people.

Twenty people from our congregation traveled three hours to San Antonio to spend the day with this church, to hear the stories, and to pray about how we should respond to this need. Our city did not have the masses

3. There was some political debate as to whether or not to call it a "crisis," however when you look at the millions of lives suffering in the balance, who seek refuge, experience violence, lose their lives, and are camped out on our border and in shelters, it should be seen as a humanitarian crisis.

of immigrants coming through it, yet we sensed the need to engage the immigration crisis that was all around us. A lack of proximity to the crisis does not excuse us from action.

In spending time with this church, we saw how one small church was extending itself on behalf of the hungry, the stranger, and the immigrant who needed shelter and care. The political narrative of the time was that murderers, rapists, and "bad hombres" were coming across our border. I cannot attest to how many come for nefarious reasons, but we knew that was not the only story to be told. We saw firsthand a different and surprising story. We heard the truly terrifying testimonies of women fleeing violence in Central America, whose husbands and sons were murdered by the cartels. With threats against their lives, they had nowhere to hide and nowhere to go but to leave their family and their country and travel the harrowing journey. The violence and danger that propels a single woman, especially with children, to make that perilous journey to get to our border is difficult to fathom.

In addition to stories of danger and violence, we heard amazing testimonies of faith. We heard of Central American pastors persecuted for their faith in God, and of families chased out of town because they stood for what was good and right. We saw women who came with their Bibles and hymnals that were given to them at their baptisms, with hardly anything else to their name. They came clinging to their faith and the hope that God would provide for their needs in a new land. We heard stories of God's presence with them in their suffering and prayers for God's deliverance along with their cries for mercy. The most surprising thing was realizing how many Christians from all over the world come to our border seeking a place of refuge and freedom. Because of the political rhetoric about immigrants, especially the stereotypes of those from Latin America, we wanted to see firsthand a different story.

Compelled by the deep faith that many from the pilgrim church bring with them, we began to realize that God was already at work around us. Could there be a God-sized invitation in this, for us as a congregation? We caught a glimpse of how in extending hospitality we participate in the work that God is already doing. We were humbled, realizing that we have so much to learn about God, God's way in the world, and our response to this reality of God's mission around us.

Many ask how a small church with limited resources might embark on such a journey of extending hospitality to women and children seeking asylum. Years of building relationships with churches and ministries in Central America laid a foundation of concern for Latin America. Years later, a family in the church opened their home to a young asylum-seeking mother with a newborn, and a team of church members gathered together, wrapping their arms around this family in support. This young mother walked from Central America to the border, pregnant and alone. The threat of violence was so real and severe that staying in her country was not an option. The permeating violence seemed to seep into every nook and cranny. She discovered that nowhere would be safe for her and her child. Once she was with us, church members helped provide rides to appointments, stopped by for visits and prayer with her, and looked for ways that she might find work. Some supported her in selling tamales; others connected her with women who might help her learn a trade. After a couple of years of this kind of support, the congregation began to dream about how it might companion other women in similar situations. Over the years, new church members have found our church because of this growing conviction. Word got out in the community that we were interested in companioning asylum seekers. Simultaneously, a small house church in Waco wanted to sell its house for use in ministry with immigrants. They contacted us and other interested people in the community for a conversation.

Our church staff, inspired by Dietrich Bonhoeffer's *Life Together* and the new-monasticism movement, nursed a dream for almost ten years of starting an intentional community in a local neighborhood where church members could share life together while extending hospitality to neighbors. While some in the congregation held this desire, others desired to walk alongside the most vulnerable in support and care. These parallel visions began to converge and work itself out in surprising ways for the congregation.

Before our church's trip to San Antonio to visit a hospitality house, we took many mission trips to Honduras and El Salvador, developing relationships with ministries there. We saw first-hand why people are compelled to leave the region. We also invited friends from these countries to our church to visit and share their stories with us. These experiences helped prepare the congregation to be receptive to what God might be calling us to do.

After a family in the church opened their home to an asylum-seeker and her baby, church members began praying for how God might be leading us. Might God be doing something among us? What is the invitation from God for us? A large cross-section of church members began meeting together for prayer and became increasingly aware that we needed and wanted to share our lives with those seeking asylum. We began to hope for a ministry where there might be a sense of complete ownership from the congregation for ministry with asylum seekers. Our planning team debated about whether to start a non-profit but ultimately landed on starting with the hospitality house being a ministry of the church, at least in the beginning. We wanted to start small, and then if it grew into something requiring non-profit status, we could adjust the model. We were warned against starting another non-profit since there is one non-profit in our town of Waco, Texas, for every 85 people. We were advised that Waco had too many non-profits. The planning team wanted to be all in and hands-on in ministry with asylum seekers. Of course, we all had appropriate reservations and fears and wrestled with, "This is too much. How can we do this? Do we want to be so consumed?" These are all very valid and important concerns we continue to consider and address. One of our church mottos has been "many hands make light work," a phrase we hear each year when church members sign up to serve in the church in some capacity. We have adopted that phrase as we talk about this ministry.

COMPANIONING AS CHRIST COMPANIONS US

Because Christ accompanies us,[4] our congregation has sought to open our hearts in accompaniment with those often overlooked and ignored, such as those seeking asylum and refuge. In our context, the Spirit of God had been moving in the congregation slowly to turn our hearts towards the needs of the marginalized. As a contemplative[5] Baptist church, the inward practices of the contemplative life began to seek an outward expression of demonstrating God's love in action. Opening our hearts to consider how the church might leave a footprint in the community was new, exciting, and terrifying. We began to ask how God might be challenging us to companion those in need.

4. In Luke 24:13–32, Jesus accompanies the disciples in their grief on the road to Emmaus. In Matt 9:19, Jesus follows the grieving father to his house. In Mark 6:47–51, Jesus walks on the water to the disciples in the boat during the storm and gets in the boat with them. Also consider God's presence with the Israelites wandering in the desert as a pillar of cloud by day and fire by night in Exod 13.

5. Our church values silence and a posture of listening for God and regularly practices contemplative prayer, such as Centering prayer, lectio divina (divine reading of Scripture) and prayers rooted in the liturgical traditions.

The concept of companioning is one of mutuality and hospitality and comes from the practice of spiritual direction. Spiritual companioning is an intentional accompanying of others through prayerful reflection and conversation that helps others notice God's work in the world. This type of contemplative spirituality has shaped our congregation in ways that have deepened both individuals' faith and the church community's relationships, resulting in an outward expression of this inner renewal. Companioning is used as a verb in this way to indicate the active commitment to a particular way of being with others.[6] Spiritual direction groups and individual spiritual direction plays an important part in the formation of the congregation and thus the language of spiritual direction has influenced our perception of how we are to engage with the world around us.

In companionship, power differentials are equalized. We as a congregation are not acting as spiritual directors in the official sense, but we approach our ministry with God's accompaniment of us in mind. While we have an active spiritual direction program in our congregation, most of those who serve in this ministry with immigrants are not involved in spiritual direction; yet the language and concepts of contemplative spirituality pervade the ethos of the congregation. I serve in a spiritual direction capacity in my ministerial role in the congregation and try to use a model of spiritual companioning with our residents in the hospitality house. The image I see when I think of a companion is one who walks with you. I remember the pillar of cloud by day and the fire by night in Exod 13, as the Spirit of God companioned the people of God through the desert. I remember Christ companioning the broken-hearted and distraught followers on the road to Emmaus. I think of the Spirit of God leading us beside still waters and walking with us through the valley of the shadow of death in the twenty-third Psalm. We often refer to what happens in spiritual direction as being a spiritual companion with another on one's journey—walking alongside someone as they seek God, reflecting with them about spiritual observations, and helping them to see God's presence in their lives.

This came full circle for me in an encounter with some of our asylum-seeking friends. On my first pastoral care visit for a new family in the hospitality house, I had been personally struggling with trying to see where God was in a painful situation in my own life. I entered the Naomi House hoping to companion our new guests and share Christ's presence with them, and they ministered to me as well. Here is an excerpt from my journal that day.

6. Reed et al., *Spiritual Companioning*, xx.

> Before walking into the Naomi House, our hospitality house for asylum seekers, for a pastoral care conversation with two new women in the home, I prayed and thought through how I might try to describe, in Spanish, the suffering Christ. These women had narrowly escaped death, slept on streets, and begged for food, all after living in hiding for a year. Their story is horrific and yet not uncommon. How could I convey that amid unspeakable suffering, Christ was with them, grieving and walking, hiding, and crying? We sat down for our visit, and I reviewed the Spanish verbs in my head, all the while trying to keep everything in the present tense. I tend to crack them up with laughter or utterly confuse them when I try to speak in the future or past. While I am sure they can use the laugh, and it is good for them to see me as deficient and needing help, I tried to find ways to convey the love of Christ with present tense conjugations.
>
> Before we could get very far, the tears started to flow and each shared how they knew that Christ was with them in their suffering. It was as clear as day to them that Christ had companioned them in their pain. They shared with me about the suffering Christ, who shared in their journey. They already knew what I wanted to share with them, and they taught me. Through lived experience, they had encountered Christ in their suffering. Buoyed by the teachings of their tiny Baptist church in the jungle of Central America, a one-room building with open-air windows and dirt floors, they had learned of Christ's suffering on the cross and how Christ walks with those who suffer.[7] They still had hurt and questions and one confessed that she was still reconciling ("reconciliando con Dios") with God. "Yo tambien, cada dia" (Me too, every day) I responded.[8]

They testified to me in full vulnerability about their grief and sorrow mingled with the assurance of Christ's presence through it. I was inspired and humbled by their deep understanding of Christ. This encounter is a perfect example of the kind of companionship we were hoping to facilitate, for they challenged and encouraged me in the middle of my anguish and struggle.

7. Liberation Theology originated in Latin America and addresses how in the suffering of the poor, those who are suffering participate and share in the same suffering as the "Suffering Servant." See Perez, "Study of Liberation Theology." For more on the tension found in seeking to understand and make sense of Latin American suffering, see Salvatierra, "Dolorisimo or Orthopathos?"

8. For more information on Latinas fleeing Central America, see the full report from the Guterres, "Women on the Run."

What Is Christian Hospitality?

The term hospitality is often deprived of its richness in popular American culture by being relegated to entertaining and dinner parties or making one's home beautiful for others to enjoy. It is easy to think of *Magnolia* and *Fixer Upper*, the TV network and home improvement and hospitality empire started by Chip and JoAnna Gains of Waco, Texas (where I also live). They have become the modern version of *Southern Living* and Martha Stewart. The giant hospitality industry in the US involves dining, travel, food, lodging, and more. Christian hospitality, however, is something altogether different. Christian hospitality has Jesus Christ at its core, who opened himself to the world for the sake of God's kingdom. Christian hospitality is about making room and extending oneself on behalf of another. It is about opening ourselves as Christ opened himself. In Christian hospitality, the stakes are high for people's souls and well-being, and sometimes even their lives are at stake. Vulnerable people sleep on our streets and wait in tents at our border. The needs of those seeking refuge and the poor can be overwhelming, and the pull of daily life often impedes offering help in these complex situations. Sharing Christian hospitality is not easy or simple; it is more than inviting a church member or a neighbor over for dinner. Hospitality has been one of the historically distinguishing traits of Christians that is at risk of becoming extinct in our fast-paced world.

It is common for people to understand the virtue of hospitality as something akin to generosity. In this understanding, hospitality is something to give or share with another. Often shared by one who has power and position, it is commonly a one-way interaction: there is a giver and a receiver. In *Dependent Rational Animals*, Alasdair MacIntyre describes virtues that humans need in order to flourish, asserting that social dependence is among the most important. He understands hospitality as grounded in "misericordia," the capacity for grief or sorrow over someone else's distress, or the ability to empathize with someone else's pain.[9] Misericordia is at the heart of hospitality and is not only an outward expression of the theological virtue of charity but a secular and moral virtue as well. MacIntyre argues that as a virtue, hospitality goes beyond sentimentality and meets the urgent needs of those who are afflicted. It extends communal relationships to those who are outside the community and is a necessary virtue for communal life. This type of empathy is the ability to share in another's situation.

9. MacIntyre, *Dependent Rational Animals*, 122–28.

Whereas some Christians relegate hospitality to creating community with other Christians (which is also important), hospitality of and with strangers is a necessity if humans are to flourish as God intends.[10]

In recent years, this type of hospitality often has not been a central part of faith expression for many Christians. It can seem to be a practice that was common in another era, but unsuitable for the modern and "dangerous" world (as if the pre-modern world were not dangerous). To reclaim hospitality as a central part of the Christian faith in this era, we must understand Christian hospitality as centered in the hospitable God, for it has always been central to the faith of those seeking God. In *Making Room: Recovering Hospitality as a Christian Tradition*, Christine Pohl makes just this point, claiming that the current use of the term hospitality has lost its moral component. She begins her book with a quote from author Henri Nouwen: "If there is any concept worth restoring to its original depth and evocative potential, it is the concept of hospitality."[11] She argues that "the possibility of receiving Jesus 'unawares' has historically intensified and influenced the practice of Christian hospitality in showing charity to the stranger."[12]

Both Joshua Jipp and Christine Pohl suggest that in hospitality the stranger becomes connected and known.[13] To be known involves deep listening and sharing, making space for one another. In this making space, the Holy Spirit shows up, connecting hearts and making way for healing and hope to emerge. This is what God longs to do in the world, to reconcile all to himself and each other. Understanding hospitality in this way underscores how essential it is for the church. Letty Russell in *Just Hospitality* describes how hospitality is more than charitable welcome. For the Christian, it is necessarily linked with justice. Quoting Pohl, she emphasizes its essential role in the Christian life: "Hospitality is not optional for Christians . . . it is a necessary practice in the community of faith."[14] Strangers are brought into the Christian community, where the Holy Spirit brings to fruition God's work of redeeming brokenness and establishing justice for a world in need of repair.

Highlighted in this book is a recent resurgence in writing on faith and hospitality that has arisen during the transition from modernity to post-modernity. I believe this resurgence has arisen for several reasons,

10. Bretherton, *Christ and the Common Life*, 274–75.

11. Pohl, *Making Room*, 3.

12. Clemot, *Discerning Welcome*, 83. See also Pohl, *Making Room*, 68.

13. Joshua Jipp, quoted in Pohl, *Making Room*, xxx.

14. Russell quotes Pohl from *Making Room*, 1.

including an overall decline of a sense of community, an epidemic of loneliness,[15] and the new era of mass migration.[16] This new era of modern mass migration shows no signs of stopping as countries struggle under the weight of corruption, economic despair, and climate-driven vulnerability. Increasingly, the church is no longer the center of North American society and suffers from a loss of credibility due to scandals and infighting. With this new wave of global mass migration, the media highlights the plight of those on the margins in both helpful and detrimental ways that keep the issue in the foreground.[17] With these converging factors, I suggest that the church recover Christian hospitality as a discipline and virtue essential to the livelihood of the church. Reclaiming hospitality can help in restoring the reputation of the church and highlight its call to be a light in the darkness, living out values that at times seem to be counter to that of the prevailing culture.

While many North American Christians may not define their Christian identity as one of a homeless foreigner, this theme is an important part of the Christian faith found in Scripture, which often has been overlooked and neglected by those in the West. In the Old Testament, the people of God were sojourners and refugees, on a journey of migration with God as their guide. For a generation, they were homeless migrants.[18] Based on Israel's own experience, caring for the sojourner is an important part of the law of God, as found in the Old Testament.[19] Continued in the New Testament, in the second chapter of Matthew, the holy family fled violence in the middle of the night and sought safety and refuge in Egypt, which was a strange country for them. Scripture says that Christ had nowhere to lay his head (Matt 8:20), highlighting the homelessness of Christ throughout his ministry, beginning in his infancy. In Toronto, sculptor Timothy Schmaltz created a visual translation of this verse, depicting Jesus as a homeless person sleeping on a park bench with a blanket over him.[20] Rosemary Radford Ruether describes Jesus's homelessness as kenosis, or the voluntary

15. US Health and Human Services, "New Surgeon General Advisory."

16. St. Johns, "New Wave of Mass Migration."

17. For example, PBS News, "Climate Change." See this example for a more negative and nuanced approach Edlow, "Biden's 'Abolish ICE Agenda.'"

18. Num 32:13; Exod 16:35, 17:1–16; Ps 107:4–6; Jer 2:6, Josh 14:10.

19. Exod 12:49, 22:21–24, 23:9; Lev 19:34, Deut 24:14.

20. See Schmaltz's sculpture here: http://www.sculpturebytps.com/about-the-artist/.

renunciation of power for the purpose of submitting to God's will.[21] In many ways, our Christian vocation is also one of kenosis, of giving up power for the sake of submitting to God's ultimate purposes. Understanding Christ's kenosis and embracing the heritage of God's faithfulness amidst a people who were without place and home should impact how Christians today interact with the issues of foreigners, the homeless, and those who are seeking asylum and safety.

Hospitality and community are ultimately modeled for us by the Godhead. Existing in community, the Trinity: Father, Son, and Holy Spirit, offer community to all who will receive. God in holy hospitality created humankind for the purpose of communion with the Divine. Christ's hospitality, outstretched arms, his opening of himself to the world created space for God's healing work to happen. By submitting to God's will and plan, Christ gathered all in, creating community as he ministered along the way, sharing the gift of reconciliation with the world. Christ's life demonstrates that hospitality is necessarily redemptive and communal, and thus core to the Christian faith. The Holy Spirit at Pentecost brought people together, empowered and transcended cultures and languages so that all might understand and share in the community that was forming.

Letty Russell describes four components of biblical hospitality: the unexpected divine presence, advocacy for the marginalized, mutual welcome, and creation of community.[22] In demonstrating biblical hospitality we can encounter God's presence in unexpected ways, and we are drawn to advocate for our friends. In these friendships, mutuality and reciprocity grow and Christian community begins to develop. In connecting action and reflection, she suggests that "just (as in justice-seeking) hospitality" pays thoughtful consideration to power imbalances and seeks truthful confession and resistance to division. "The sort of hospitality that makes this possible would be one that sees the struggle for justice as part and parcel of welcoming the stranger."[23]

For our congregation, extending hospitality is participation in God's justice, sharing our lives with those whose "backs are against the wall," as Howard Thurman puts it.[24] It is part of what it means to be co-laborers with God in God's kingdom that is unfolding this side of heaven. It is

21. Perkins, *Practice in Christianity*, 328.

22. Russell, *Just Hospitality*, 82–88.

23. Russell, *Just Hospitality*, xv.

24. Thurman, *Jesus and the Disinherited*.

important to note that hospitality should be disentangled from power, as it should require nothing in return. Hospitality is relational and empathetic, creating space for mutuality, and in this space, reciprocity can emerge, but it is never required nor coerced. Luke Bretherton describes hospitality as a virtue necessary for living in a pluralistic society. It is not to be confused with philanthropy, which often has undercurrents of those with power and position giving to those on the "outside." It is not one-sided but makes room for commonality. In hospitality, commonality and mutuality are discovered,[25] differences diminish, and connections emerge. Lives that once existed in different worlds and countries discover friendship and a shared faith in God. Families from one culture find common interests with a family from another while sharing a meal. New recipes shared and received build bridges between cultures, forging new friendships. Common meaning emerges as we connect on the most basic of human levels, when we connect through our shared humanity.

I see this most often in shared worship. Some of our new friends and church members from Central America who are asylum seekers have contributed to our worshiping community. Once a month we have a night of singing in Spanish in our hospitality house, with guitars and ukuleles, an occasional violin, and songs in Spanish from different countries where our new friends lift their voices in praise along with long-time church members. During this time, we also practice some of the common choruses and hymns sung in our worship service as well as the liturgy so that they can fully participate. Conversely, our talented friends also lead our congregation in worship in Spanish some during Sunday morning worship, at church fellowships, and on Wednesday evenings with our young people. Multi-national worship opens the door for commonality and mutuality. Barriers and walls come down and we all become equals as we learn to worship together in different languages.

In one visit with guests in the Naomi House, I was personally processing a grief in which I struggled to see how God could redeem the pain a loved one had suffered, nor could I see where God was amidst that pain. I was at the Naomi House to pray with and encourage our guests. As I spoke with the woman, she shared with me how she was clinging to the knowledge in her head that God was with her through her painful journey and trauma, but at the same time she was still working things out with God. She and God

25. Bretherton, *Christ and the Common Life*, 16. For more on Bretherton and hospitality, see Bretherton, *Hospitality as Holiness*.

had unfinished business, and she was living in that tension. It was a moment of reminder for me that I too can and do live in that tension. She gave a gift of encouragement to me that day. Another young asylum-seeking woman from our ministry has been so impacted by the ministry that she wanted to find a way to give back to me. When she got into a housing situation of her own, one of her first acts was to invite me into her house for a meal. I had to make space for these reversals of hospitality, and I joyfully realized that I was on the receiving end of hospitality. I opened myself in vulnerability to relationships with these women, ready to receive with gracious thanksgiving the gifts that they shared with me. Reciprocity is part of biblical hospitality, where mutual giving and receiving take place.

Luke 24 describes Cleopas and his companion walking from Jerusalem to Emmaus on Resurrection Sunday. They spoke of all that had happened with Christ's execution and the empty tomb. Bewildered, they encountered a stranger on the dusty road. Christ, the sojourner, walked with the travelers, *accompanying* them. Not recognizing Jesus, Cleopas called him a stranger and then explained with a downcast face all their hopes and disappointment. They had hoped that Jesus Christ would be the Messiah, but he had been killed and his body was now missing. In their confusion and bewilderment, these travelers then extended hospitality, as they had been taught, to Christ the foreigner or outsider, while still unable to see that he was the Christ. They invited Christ, the outsider, into their home. It was only then, in the breaking of bread and sharing of a meal that Christ revealed himself. In a strange reversal, Christ the guest became host. Christian hospitality demonstrates mutuality and a commonly shared meaning. Eventually, hospitality involves reciprocity, so that the one opening and extending hospitality also opens to receiving it when it is offered back. So too, the guest becomes the one who gives, they become the host. Contrary to popular opinion, hospitality has at its core a sense of mutuality and respect that empowers the receiver to become a giver. This is what distinguishes it from philanthropy.

Hospitality is the love of the stranger or *philoxenia* in Greek, as opposed to xenophobia, which is fear of strangers. We partner with Christ in *koinonia* (Christian fellowship) to extend hospitality, thus sharing the hospitable God with others. All this is for the sake of God's kingdom on earth, as we regularly pray in the Lord's Prayer: *thy kingdom come, thy will be done, on earth as it is in heaven*. Hospitality often takes on the virtues of justice and mercy, which is traditionally understood as giving what is not due or compassionate treatment of those in distress. Hospitality is taking in an orphan or an immigrant who has suffered violence and has nowhere to go; it is mercy that seeks to try to make things right. While hospitality cannot fix all problems, being brought into community or fellowship, receiving mercy, and being accompanied assist in making situations more just. It is part of extending the love and peace of Christ to all in practical ways. Each Sunday at the end of worship, we share the peace of Christ with the neighbor sitting next to us in worship, practicing how we are to engage with the world as we walk out the doors. This is part of what it means to be the hands and feet of Christ in this place. Thus, Christian hospitality is directly linked to mercy, which is a form of justice, with those who suffer.

The parable of the great feast in Luke 14:12–24 describes the kingdom of God as a feast in which the poor, the lame, and those on the margins of society are brought into table fellowship and friendship. In this passage, all those who suffer, are welcomed into the community. All are offered a seat at the table of feasting in God's kingdom. Such hospitality brings others into community, offering relationships and the opportunity to seek God together.

Baptist theologian Elizabeth Newman defines hospitality as the Christian practice in which we meet God. She states that hospitality is "our participation in what God is doing."[26] Hospitality is not about benevolent giving so much as joining God and participating in God's work, and in so doing, we are changed. Like the travelers on the road to Emmaus were changed after inviting Christ into the home and breaking bread with him, so we expectantly seek God's transformation in our own lives. As will be seen in the pages that follow, this understanding of hospitality reflects the early church's approach to Christian hospitality.

Western culture tends to seek insulation and protection.[27] This avoidance of suffering inhibits our ability and desires to "be the hands and feet of Christ." The old are sent to nursing homes, with the mentality that someone else will take care of all who do not fit the norm of society. Parents protect their children from consequences, despite the reality that consequences might be good for their well-being.[28] Some want to not teach about the

26. Newman, *Untamed Hospitality*, 60.

27. For more on this see Ji et al., "Cultural Differences," 1039–47.

28. A quick Google search on overprotective parenting yields many results on the dangers of protecting children too much and the importance of allowing them to face the consequences of their actions.

history of racism in our country because it could cause discomfort to children. Others think that suffering occurs because of a fault or personal shortcoming. This plays itself out in issues of the poor and the immigrant. Consciously and unconsciously, some think that the plight of the poor and the immigrants stems from personal failures to manage money or resources, to associate with the wrong people, or to not work hard enough. These judgments then prevent us from engaging, from serving, and thus from meeting Christ in their midst. Additionally, in our culture that prioritizes self-preservation, the "problem" of suffering can be one of many issues that lead to a falling away from the faith in our younger generations.[29] By avoiding suffering, we have sent the message to younger generations that suffering is a punishment from God or that Christ cannot be found in the suffering but only in the blessing. This leaves a faith that can appear hollow, and has resulted in the church demonstrating a lack of credibility. This tendency to avoid suffering has infiltrated North American churches, as many remain siloed behind stained glass windows, from the suffering of the least of these in the world, lacking a clear mission to comfort the afflicted. Reclaiming the early church's understanding of suffering can enliven our faith and strengthen the church to meet the challenges of the twenty-first century.

Who Is the Asylum Seeker?

Much information has been produced in recent years about immigration, migration, refugees, and asylum seekers. According to the latest studies, there were 304 million global migrants in 2024, which is almost four percent of the world's population. As of 2020, the number of people living outside their origin countries was at its historical high and more migrants chose the US as their destination than any other country.[30] Famine, war, violence, ineffective governments, lack of gainful employment, and natural disasters are all reasons that cause someone to flee their home country. The United Nations High Commission on Refugees (UNHCR) is the United Nations advocacy arm for refugees who are forcibly displaced; they provide

29. See Bodenner, "Losing Your Faith," and Thornton, "What Causes People to Lose Their Faith?"

30. Batalova, "Top Statistics on Global Migration" and migrationpolicy.org.

a wealth of data on global migration while also tracking individual trends and aid for refugees.[31]

Pending asylum cases have reached an all-time high in the US, with nearly 1.6 million cases awaiting determination in the courts.[32] During the 2022 fiscal year, 25,465 refugees were admitted to the US, which *Statista* has tracked since 1990 when 125,000 refugees were admitted to the United States in one year.[33] Conversely, the number of asylum seekers grew from 8,472 in 1990 to 30,964 in 2020 along with rises in border apprehensions.[34] This drastic increase reflects the reality of the dawning era of mass migration of people not officially considered "refugees" and demands a new response to this critical predicament.[35] In recent years, immigrants fleeing the Northern Triangle (Honduras, Guatemala, and El Salvador) were the majority of immigrants reaching the southern border. In 2023, however, more migrants have come from South America due to unrest in the region.[36] The year 2022 broke previous records of undocumented migrants crossing the southern US border, topping 2.76 million people.[37] The statistics, policies, terminology, and rhetoric can be confusing. The asylum seekers, who have little recourse, are just one subset of immigrants. They are not afforded refugee status and, therefore, seek asylum and safety through the formal asylum request process as outlined by the US government. The United Nations has long held that it is a fundamental right to seek asylum and advocates for this right worldwide. After the atrocities of World War II, when thousands of Jews were denied asylum in America, the world began to change its views on asylum-seeking, and international asylum laws were established.[38]

Refugees, who are often in imminent danger of losing their lives if they stay in their home country,[39] are often afforded refugee status by the

31. For more information on global trends, see the United Nations' World Migration Report (2002).

32. Syracuse University TRAC Immigration, "Sober Assessment."

33. Statista, "Number of Refugee Admissions."

34. USA Facts, "How Many People Seek Asylum in the US?"

35. See my article in the Waco Tribune Herald, Harris, "Building Stronger Communities."

36. For more information, see Gramlich, "Monthly Encounters."

37. Ainsley, "Migrant Border Crossings."

38. For more information, see the Southern Poverty Law Center and the National Holocaust Museum.

39. Clemot, *Discerning Welcome*, 7.

UN High Court on Refugees (or Convention on Refugees). Many asylum seekers who present themselves at the border or a port of entry have similar threats of danger, however most of them are not granted the status of refugee. Traditionally, an asylum seeker must present a credible threat[40] at the border to be allowed into the country to pursue the legal means to seek asylum. Once in the country, asylum seekers must file a request for asylum with the courts within one year. If that official request is not filed in court within one year, they lose the opportunity to seek asylum and thus are deemed to be here illegally. Essentially the only difference between refugees and asylum seekers is where they apply for their status. Asylum seekers apply at a port of entry whereas refugees apply for and receive the status before they arrive in their country of resettlement.[41]

A refugee and an asylum seeker both have paths to citizenship if they are granted resident alien status. If they are not granted this status, then they must leave the country or stay and risk deportation. For an asylum seeker, this process can take 3–5 years.[42] Our congregation chose to companion Latina asylum-seekers because they seemed to be the most vulnerable of all immigrants. Refugees often have some funding and support that follows them through immigration and refugee services, whereas asylum-seekers do not. Women and children seeking asylum at the southern border are at risk for trafficking and exploitation by predatory organizations, workplaces, and individuals.

As Bretherton asserts, a key factor in determining refugee status is the presence of persecution that is personal in nature and precisely political.[43] Many immigrants endure personal or political persecution but are not granted refugee or asylum status for a myriad of reasons. It can be hard to prove political or personal persecution and distinguish it from regional violence and unstable governments. If an immigrant does not have good legal representation or support in navigating the legal system, their case may not receive appropriate consideration.

Two common misconceptions about immigrants often prevent the church from engaging in ministry with those living on the margins, who have lost their rights and community. First, there is a misconception that

40. American Immigration Council, "Asylum in the United States."

41. González, *Beyond Welcome*, xii.

42. At the time of writing, the legal asylum process can take 3–5 years. For more information, see Rescue.org's article, "Is It Legal to Cross the U.S. Border to Seek Asylum?"

43. Bretherton, *Christianity and Contemporary Politics*, 128.

anyone coming to the southern border is coming illegally. Political rhetoric often deliberately demonizes this vulnerable population, stoking fear and inaccurately spreading disinformation.[44] Currently[45] the only way for an immigrant to apply for asylum status is to present themselves at a border or port of entry requesting asylum, and to provide evidence of credible threat at that time. Border agents then decide if they will grant entry into the US so they may then apply to have their case heard in court.[46] Second, another misconception about immigrants is that they are draining "the system" and not paying taxes. However, they do pay sales tax, income tax (once they have work permits), and property tax via rent payments. These myths about immigration and the cultivation of prejudice against immigrants contribute to indifference toward alleviating and addressing this unique kind of suffering. It is important to dispel these misconceptions and prejudice as a way of empowering the church to look squarely at the suffering, to lament the suffering, and then to seek the hope of Christ in it. In facing the darkness of the suffering of immigrants, and in facing the hard truth of the plight of asylum-seekers, Christ's light then has a chance to shine and speak into those places of lament and bring redemption. We cannot be the hands and feet of Christ in this way without clearly seeing the reality of the lament.

"Bare Life" and Hallowing

In *Christianity and Contemporary Politics*, Luke Bretherton describes the refugee as one functioning in "bare life."[47] By this, he means a person who is reduced to life only, with no other rights as a human being. Refugees and asylum seekers often live in fear. They are devoid of some rights (rights commonly afforded to a citizen), living a life that is excluded or banned from participation in society, having no country to claim as their own. They are repeatedly exposed to death and danger, and they are devalued.[48] Bretherton argues that Christian cosmopolitanism *sees*, or bears witness to, the immigrant and the varying needs of each subset of immigrants (refugee, asylum-seeker, others). Each of these embodies "bare life," or dehumanization,

44. Abdelkader, "Immigration in the Era of Trump."

45. At the time of this writing, as immigration laws are constantly changing and being challenged.

46. U.S. Citizenship and Immigration Services, "Obtaining Asylum in the United States."

47. Bretherton is relying upon the work of Giorgio Agamben: *Homo Sacer*.

48. Bretherton, *Christianity and Contemporary Politics*, 138–39.

and Christian cosmopolitanism seeks constructive ways to address their gaping needs. Bretherton additionally assesses the practice of sanctuary and the US sanctuary movement as one way of addressing immigrants in their bare life, and a way of living out Christian cosmopolitanism.

John Calvin noted that the whole human race is to be received with charity and to be viewed not in themselves but in God.[49] This echoes the early church's understanding of seeing Christ in the other, of seeing in others the *imago Dei* (the image of God). Hallowing God's name, as laid out in the Lord's Prayer, can be demonstrated in hallowing bare life, in standing up for and against all that desecrates God's name. To hallow, one must see and notice, to honor. Hallowing the suffering and the "bare life" of those on the margins, since they are the *imago Dei*, is to hallow God's name. One way the church hallows or honors God's name is by involving itself with refugees, as those who bear the image of God.[50] Hallowing can mean "to summon forth" and "to bless or sanctify," to make holy and set apart. The church can respond to refugees by blessing and summoning forth.[51] The church can welcome immigrants into fellowship and community and can bless them with relationships and support by walking alongside them in mutuality.

As Bretherton puts it, the "involvement of churches with refugees should be characterized as the hallowing of bare life . . . intrinsic to the command to hallow the name of God (Exod 20:1–7)."[52] Churches that open themselves to giving and receiving hospitality with asylum seekers are putting into practice the hallowing of God's name as expressed in the beginning of the Lord's Prayer: "Our Father, in heaven, hallowed be your name, your kingdom come, your will be done, on earth as it is in heaven" (Matt 6:9–10 NIV).

For Augustine, the earthly city negotiates peace so that the gospel can be shared, God can be worshiped, and communion with God happens. This lays the groundwork for human flourishing.[53] Calvin states that all are to be viewed "in God," meaning that Christian charity is extended to all peoples regardless of distinction.[54] Karl Barth goes further to state that patriotism

49. Bretherton, *Christianity and Contemporary Politics*, 132.

50. Bretherton, *Christianity and Contemporary Politics*, 145.

51. Bretherton, *Christianity and Contemporary Politics*, 145.

52. Bretherton, *Christianity and Contemporary Politics*, 145.

53. Bretherton, *Christianity and Contemporary Politics*, 135.

54. Bretherton, *Christianity and Contemporary Politics*, 132.

should not be narrow, but citizens must direct their gaze and energy to the "good of the whole human family."[55] Writing specifically about the United Kingdom, Anna Rowlands expands on this idea of society seeking the common good, especially in terms of migration and immigration. She highlights how both the political left and right have also used the term "common good" in recent years while neglecting the political foundations in which human flourishing can happen.[56] In a rationalist cosmopolitanism, the genre of tracts called *Catéchèse de humanité* of the late eighteenth century, instructed the French public in their duties of brotherhood of mankind, highlighting respect for all of humanity over and above regional loyalty.[57] The duty of care for mankind is not only a Christian trait but one that is esteemed by non-Christian writers as well, and which is seeing a resurgence in rhetoric, even if policies that promote it may be lacking.

Christian Hospitality

Many have written eloquently on welcome, hospitality, immigration, and the role of the church at these intersections. I highlight the following books as important contributions and viewpoints for those seeking to broaden their understanding of Christian hospitality. These are helpful resources for any congregation looking to equip themselves for a ministry of hospitality. In *Making Room*, Christine Pohl approaches hospitality as a way of life fundamental to the Christian identity,[58] and her experience was often with people who found themselves at the margins of society. She does not shy away from the difficulties of practicing this type of hospitality, and she offers ideas for how to recover the ancient practice while highlighting communities that are already doing so. *Just Hospitality* by Letty Russell is a posthumous compilation of her lectures and writings on hospitality, based upon her reflections on years of table fellowship.

Joshua Jipp in *Saved by Faith and Hospitality*[59] bases his book on Scripture and the early Christian book of 1 Clement, in which the ancient author makes the claim that Abraham, Lot, and Rahab were saved by both their faith and their hospitality. While this may be a controversial statement

55. Bretherton, *Christianity and Contemporary Politics*, 132.

56. Rowlands, "Politics of the Common Good," 37–51.

57. Bretherton, *Christianity and Contemporary Politics*, 133.

58. Pohl, *Making Room*, x.

59. Jipp and Pohl, *Saved by Faith and Hospitality*.

today about salvation, it suggests that hospitality is part and parcel of the Christian faith (Jas 2:14–26; Matt 7:19–23). Protestants believe works or faith in action are not salvific but are an outward expression of faith and salvation. The Christian faith is rooted in the hospitable God. Amy Oden's book *And You Welcomed Me*[60] is a sourcebook on hospitality in the early church that highlights stories and teachings on hospitality and care for strangers from early Christian writers, church fathers, and saints. She uses a wealth of primary texts to make her point about the primacy of hospitality to the early church, and her questions for group discussion might be a good resource for small groups.

Pope Francis in *A Stranger and You Welcomed Me*[61] offers a collection of stories and sermons on immigration, urging Christians to look at and address the root causes of migration, reminding all that Jesus and his family were refugees in Egypt. Priscilla Sun Kyung Oh in *Hospitable Witnessing*[62] understands hospitality as bearing witness to what God is doing, and shares about hospitality from the perspective of friendship amidst mental illness. Edward Smither in *Mission as Hospitality*[63] seeks to reclaim hospitality as an essential part of Christian missional engagement with the "not-yet people of God" as a way of making room for others while also proclaiming the gospel.

Ellen Clark Clemot in *Discerning Welcome* offers a Reformed faith perspective from personal experience of her church extending hospitality and sanctuary to the immigrant. Peter Meilaender in *Toward a Theory of Immigration*[64] and Luke Bretherton in *Christ and the Common Life* address theology and immigration from a theological and political perspective. Elizabeth Newman in *Untamed Hospitality* offers a theological account of hospitality rooted in Christian worship. Luke Bretherton's *Hospitality as Holiness: Christian Witness Amid Moral Diversity* offers hospitality as the shape of Christian witness, which is grounded in Alasdair MacIntyre's assessment of the contemporary context in conversation with Oliver O'Donovan's distinctiveness of Christian ethics.

60. Oden, *And You Welcomed Me.*

61. Francis, *Stranger and You Welcomed Me.*

62. Oh, *Hospitable Witnessing.*

63. Smither, *Mission as Hospitality.*

64. Meilaender, *Toward a Theory of Immigration.*

M. Daniel Carroll R. in *The Bible and Borders*[65] compiles a comprehensive biblical overview of hospitality throughout the Bible, which is an essential primer to use in a congregational setting or as a small group study with congregants wanting to learn more about what the Bible has to say about immigration. Similarly, Stephan Bauman and co-authors Isaam Simeir and Matthew Soerens, President of World Relief, in *Seeking Refuge*,[66] seek to equip Christians and churches to be able to address the global refugee crisis and is geared towards a more evangelical audience.

There are many other ways in which Christians seek to address the issues of immigration and specifically refugees and asylum seekers from non-profit organizations in many denominations (such as Lutheran Refugee Services and Catholic Charities) to non-governmental organizations (International Rescue Committee and the UNHCR are two that are not faith-based), all of which are great resources and partners in ministry with the asylum seeker. Some churches and denominations operate welcome houses (Welcome House Network and Welcome House Raleigh or the Mennonite Community Hospitality House network and Catholic Worker Houses), while some individual congregations offer their grounds and buildings as sanctuary, a place of refuge and safety from deportation. The short documentary *Santuario*[67] is a good place to begin exploring how a church might engage in hospitality in this way.

Why the Church Needs Ministry with Those on the Margins Like Asylum Seekers

There is no shortage of books and articles on how the church in North America is on the decline, that we are entering a post-Christian age, and that young people are leaving the faith like never before.[68] I have heard concerned elders from "the greatest generation" express dismay and worry about the future of the church for their great-grandchildren. Much of the

65. Carroll R., *Bible and Borders.*

66. Bauman et al., *Seeking Refuge.* See also *Welcoming the Stranger* by Soerens.

67. See the promo website, http://www.santuariofilm.com/about. See also Isaac Villegas's YouTube lecture, "Providing Sanctuary as Witness."

68. Barna Group, "Atheism Doubles Among Generation Z." Bolsinger, *Canoeing the Mountains.* See also Thornton, "What Causes People to Lose Their Faith?" See also Jones, *End of White Christian America*; Burge, "Only Half of Kids"; also Silliman, "Decline of Christianity."

political and ecclesiological rhetoric from evangelicals today is about preserving the declining church. A Google search will pull up "save the church in North America" and website after website devoted to this topic. More internet searching will quickly discover five ways and ten ideas, twenty keys, and many more posts about how to "save" the declining church, with evangelists devoted solely to this purpose. Pollsters, media pundits, pastors, magazines, and news organizations all devote many articles, opinions, and commentaries to this matter.

Society is in the middle of a sea change—a change of culture and values, of environment and climate, of stability—a change of how we get and understand information, and all of this means a change for the Church. There is a popular story of a man who was drowning in a flood. He prayed fervently for the Lord to save his life and begged God for mercy and help. Eventually, a boat came by and asked if the man needed help, and the man told the boat captain that he did not need any help because he knew the Lord would save him. It is a common, well-told story. Another boat came by, and then a helicopter came by. All the while the man about to drown told the rescuers no, that he was waiting on God to rescue him. The story ends with the man drowning, refusing the help that was sent to him by God.

A group of twenty from our congregation traveled to San Antonio to learn from our sisters and brothers in the faith of how God was calling them and using them in a ministry of hospitality, justice, and mercy with the immigrant. While there, Pastor John Garland prophetically told our team, "The pilgrim church is coming our way; are we willing to receive them?" He challenged our congregation to consider how we might extend hospitality to asylum seekers—those who are some of the most vulnerable in society.

After all the talk and prayers about the North American church's decline, the *nones*,[69] churches closing their doors, and young people leaving, could it be possible that the very answer to these prayers is the pilgrim church arriving at our border? I am not talking about immigrants adding numbers to declining church attendance. It is the perspective of immigrants, their experiences with God, and their faith that the North American church needs. Christianity is growing in the Global South, and it is this church, on the move fleeing persecution and violence, and seeking freedom that is coming to our borders. The North American church has so much to learn from Christians in the Global South. They come bringing a tested

69. Lipka, "Closer Look."

faith, a daily dependence upon God, and a true understanding of suffering and faith that today's church can benefit from. They could be the very thing that God uses to reinvigorate the North American church. The catch is that Christians must be willing to let them in, to open hearts, homes, lives, and churches to them. Humility is a choice and must be embraced. Todd Bolsinger, in *Canoeing the Mountains*, describes leadership in the church in this era as "off the map" (post-post-modernity, post-Christendom). It is a time to listen to marginal voices, those who have been silenced, and learn from them.[70] The church is "off the map" navigating uncharted waters of a post-Christendom society, and the pilgrim church has come.

The North American church risks being like the man in the flood, turning away the boats and the helicopter, not realizing that the boats and the helicopter were God's ways of answering prayers for rescue. The boats for our rescue may be the pilgrim church, knocking on our borders. I in no way want to minimize the great suffering of those seeking refuge and asylum, nor am I suggesting that God has caused this crisis that has led to mass migration. I am offering, however, that in it, God is working, healing, and reconciling. The North American church has an opportunity to experience Christ in this crisis. The people of God have always been a pilgrim people, whose allegiance is to God above and beyond any human or political agenda. Christians have been called by God to deny ourselves, take up our cross, and follow Christ (Mark 8:34–35) to the "least of these" (Matt 25:34–40). One Central American woman told her pastor, "If I flee and even make it to America, where will I go? Who will help me?" Her pastor told her, "Don't worry, just get to America, the church will help you."

Will we? Many Spanish-speaking churches across the country and along the border are doing extraordinary work in this area along with some small Anglo churches in certain pockets. It is work that more of us can do, that we need to do, for our own souls, and for the restoration of the church in North America today.

The church has an opportunity to step out and embrace the pilgrim church at our border. Many of these immigrants come clinging to their faith and their hope in Jesus Christ. They have experienced violence that many of us will never know, and yet they still have faith. We have so much to learn from them. Our youngest generations are leaving the faith, often because of issues of hypocrisy, reconciling evil and pain with the idea of God as good, and the irrelevance of the religion and faith. Learning and

70. Bolsinger, *Canoeing the Mountains*, 189–203.

listening from the pilgrim church just might be the help we need to see afresh the essentials of our faith.

Ora et labora is the traditional Benedictine mantra meaning prayer and work. This does not mean pray and then work but rather prayer becomes one's work and work becomes one's prayer. Serving God in our actions is our prayer. This has been a guiding phrase in our congregation for a long time and permeates our hospitality ministry. Ministry with the asylum seeker is one way we worship and participate in God's inbreaking kingdom on earth. We are co-laborers with God in this endeavor. It is work that transforms our own hearts as we meet God in the stranger and our lives are changed. As we work, we pray and experience God's transformation.

Building a Ministry

I have just laid the foundation of terms of hospitality and asylum seeker and described briefly the background for this book. In the following chapters, I offer a formation guide for starting a hospitality house for asylum seekers as a part of a church's ministry in the community. Congregations can engage in hands-on ministry with immigrants and others in need in many faithful ways, thus enacting Christ's instructions in Matthew 25.[71] Here, I describe one way a congregation has sought to greet strangers as if they are Christ. Since I describe a process for opening a hospitality house for asylum seekers, I use the image and terminology for building a house throughout the book. Although we did not physically build a house, we did build a ministry in a house, on land that also needed renewal, as did those who came to the house in search of healing and hope. In many ways, it was an exercise in the reclamation of land and souls, and a stubborn act of hope, trusting that God would show up.

Chapter 2 is about equipping the leader, and chapter 3 is about equipping the congregation, both laying out important theological and ecclesiological preparation for leading a congregation in this type of ministry. They are foundational chapters for building a hospitality ministry. For most small and mid-size congregations, embarking upon a ministry of this sort does not happen overnight. There is a lot of groundwork that needs to happen theologically to reach the point of willingness to consider opening a hospitality house for asylum seekers. Our church, with varied political and

71. Matt 25:35 NIV: "For I was hungry, and you gave me something to eat, I was thirsty, and you gave me something to drink, I was a stranger and you invited me in."

theological perspectives, did this; a strong foundation was essential. Hospitality ministry to the vulnerable asylum seeker stands on the tradition of the church and is an extension of ways, throughout history, in which Christians through the church have sought to deny themselves and follow Christ (Mark 8).

In chapter 2, "Equipping the Leader," I provide a brief overview of the Church's ministry of mercy, justice, and hospitality, beginning with the early church through the present. This background equips pastors and church leaders to have strong pastoral and theological standing as they lead their congregations.

In chapter 3, "Equipping the Congregation," I propose a biblical study and overview of immigration and hospitality throughout the Bible, ending with a section on current events and resources. This is an outline of a basic study through which a congregation can journey. I do not recreate the in-depth Bible study that is already available on this issue through multiple books and resources, but rather provide a possible outline for a study series that the reader can flesh out more clearly to fit the needs of their congregation.

Overall, chapters 2 and 3 address the question, "How do you prepare leaders and congregations for a ministry of hospitality?" by looking at theological and educational preparation to lay a strong foundation for a ministry of this sort.

In the second half of the book, I turn to the everyday and quotidian, seeking to address challenges and typical questions that emerge. This is where I get immensely practical and tackle some of the details of hospitality ministry.

Next, chapter 4, "Nuts and Bolts of Developing a Ministry," describes how one congregation did it. I address vocation and calling and how we structured our hospitality house. I also describe how we trained our congregation for this work.

Finally, chapter 5, "Maintaining a Ministry and Thriving," addresses the challenges and skills that were called forth amidst this endeavor. I do not claim to be a master at this, but I describe our experiences and how we processed them. Humility is a common theme that unites all of what we experienced and tried to practice.

I conclude in chapter 6, "Bearing Witness: A Theological and Pastoral Reflection," with a summary and reflection on what it means to bear witness to the work of God among us. I apply *The Word Made Flesh Model*,[72] which seeks to identify where we were going, identify the lament, and claim the hope.

72. Balmaceda, "Word Made Flesh."

2

Equipping the Leader

ANYTIME ONE BUILDS A house or a structure, laying the foundation is one of the first steps. It is common knowledge that without a strong and well-laid foundation, a house or building will not withstand the challenges of age and climate. Similarly, a strong foundation is crucial to sensing God's calling and beginning to put into action a ministry of hospitality.

Following the introduction to "building" a hospitality house in chapter 1, this and the next two chapters continue the construction metaphor: "Laying the Foundation," "Beginning and Blueprints," "Framing and Setting the Structure," and "Maintaining the House." In two main parts, "Equipping the Minister" and "Equipping the Congregation," this chapter addresses the questions, "How do you prepare the leaders for a ministry of hospitality?" and "How do you prepare the congregation for a ministry of hospitality?"

We live in an age of confused, weaponized, and distorted information. Some call it misinformation or multiple truths. Our facts and your facts, your truth, and my truth. This is the environment in which churches must learn to navigate and find new ways to extend the loving embrace of God to those on the margins and specifically to the asylum seeker who receives so much disdain. One way we can equip congregations is by remembering our history and the ancient call of Christ and the church to greet the stranger as if they are Christ. The next section seeks to inform and correct misinformed ideas of what the Bible and church history have to say about caring for the outsider.

PASTORAL AND THEOLOGICAL PREPARATION FOR LEADERS

First, a brief overview of the church's ministry of mercy, justice, and hospitality beginning with the early church through the present. I address how the church has historically engaged with hospitality and mercy. It provides an essential foundation for the entire endeavor of opening a hospitality house. This historical background equips pastors and church leaders to have strong pastoral and theological standing as they lead their congregations and address the question, "How do you prepare leaders for a ministry of hospitality?"

Hospitality and Mercy to Sufferers: The Church's Response Through History

Church history has much to teach the modern church about ministry and mission, and about teaching and making disciples. For many, however, it is easy to overlook the witness of the early church or to dismiss it as being outdated and irrelevant. Nevertheless, the witness of the church throughout time is instructive and can offer great insights into some of the challenges that the global church faces today. Kavin Rowe, in *Christianity's Surprise*,[1] argues that the early church grew exponentially, in part, due to the ways in which they embraced those who suffered by establishing hospitals and caring for the poor, the sick, the widow, and the orphan. They were able to do this because they faced their own suffering and saw in "the other" the *imago Dei*. Their understanding of seeing Christ in others was a result of their deep theological training and teaching ministry. Recapturing this understanding can have important implications for the church today and informs how the church can engage in justice ministry. Rowe's work directly ties the growth of the early church to their engagement with what we might call today "social justice ministry" as expressly rooted in their understanding of Christ and theology.

Additionally, Leo Lefebure in his article on the understanding of suffering in the early church explores how the early church attempted to interpret the origin of suffering. Suffering for the early church became instructive and an opportunity to learn and grow in Christlikeness.[2] K. C.

1. Rowe, *Christianity's Surprise*.
2. Lefebure, "Understanding of Suffering," 29–37.

Richardson in *Early Christian Care for the Poor*, highlights how the early church learned to embrace their suffering, empowering them to minister to those who suffer.[3] Not only do these have implications for ministry with those who suffer but also may address the challenge of young adults who are leaving the faith[4] due, in part, to theodicy[5] and the church's apparent lack of engagement with the real issues of hurting and marginalized people.[6, 7]

Amy Oden, in *And You Welcomed Me*,[8] recounts a story from Palladius in the fourth century as an example of one way the early church taught about hospitality.

> Elias, a hermit living in a cave, received 20 visitors one day. To offer hospitality to these strangers, he went into his cave and saw that he had only a little bit of bread. But Elias fed these strangers, giving all that he had. The remains of the bread were so plentiful that he fed himself on that bread for a month.[9]

In narrative form, this story taught Christians to give plentifully and serve freely, trusting that God will supply the increase and provide for needs as well. Oden's book is full of excerpts from primary texts from the early church highlighting the idea that the practice of hospitality was essential in the lives of early Christians. Letters and sermons were the common way for the young and growing church to instruct and establish patterns.

Hospes, the Latin word for hospitality, means welcoming the stranger. Hospitality in the Bible always refers to welcoming the foreigner and extending resources to the alien.[10] Historically, hospitality has been a moral practice but in recent years has been reduced to entertaining. In practicing hospitality, we are de-centered, and the focus shifts from self to relationships. While it is a moral discipline, it is not a private discipline but precisely communal. Contrary to our North American individualism that silos off virtue to internal or personal pursuits, hospitality is situated in the *oikos* of God, or the household of God, in God's spiritual economy. In early Christian writing, hospitality is always for the poor and the destitute, those

3. Richardson, *Early Christian Care for the Poor.*
4. Barna Group, "Atheism Doubles Among Generation Z."
5. Bodenner, "Losing Your Faith."
6. Wehner, "Evangelical Church Is Breaking Apart."
7. Thornton, "What Causes People to Lose."
8. Oden, *And You Welcomed Me*.
9. Oden, *And You Welcomed Me*, xx.
10. Oden, *And You Welcomed Me*, 13.

without "hearth, home, mattress, bed and possessions"[11] and coupled with almsgiving. These persons were commonly travelers, pilgrims, widows, orphans, slaves, and prisoners, some of whom were destitute due to war.

Tertullian argues with Marcion that the Creator God is the one who feeds the hungry and provides for the poor. Bruce Longenecker in "The Poor of Galatians 2:10," writes, "Tertullian suggests that it is this concern for the poor that causes the gentile nations to be attracted to Christianity."[12] Christians of the early church were caring for the poor with acts of hospitality in such meaningful ways that the larger culture took notice and was intrigued.

By the fourth century, hospitality to the vulnerable became ingrained in the life of the church; it was organized and institutionalized. The Didache and Apostolic Constitutions were teaching tools to help Christians know what it meant to live out their faith. Both set guidelines for the giving and receiving of hospitality. The Didache promised blessings to those who give generously to all, followed by warnings of negative consequences for those who have no mercy for the poor and who do not work on behalf of the oppressed and who turn away from those in need. Mercy and charity were a necessity.[13] In the fourth century, Christians were beginning to organize themselves around the sharing of hospitality by establishing structures and institutions to maintain this important ministry. Hospitals and hospices were founded, and safe houses for strangers, widows, and orphans began emerging.

Although the "stranger" and circumstances today may be different, Andy Hogue and Greg Jones in *Navigating the Future* challenge leaders to learn from tradition and then allow for room for innovation.[14] Their work prepares leaders to expound upon current understandings and practices of leadership. When applied to the Christian discipline of hospitality with the stranger, Christian leaders can easily expand the ancient practice of hospitality to include immigrants seeking asylum today.

11. Gregory of Nyssa, "As You Did It To One of These," in Oden, *And You Welcomed Me*, 22.

12. Longenecker and Liebengood, *Engaging Economics*, 210.

13. Rhee, *Loving the Poor*, 135.

14. Hogue and Jones, *Navigating the Future*.

How the Christian Church Changed the View and Response to Suffering

As shown in the following quote, early Christians distinguished themselves from the Greco-Roman world as people expressly interested in the poor. They noticed the poor when the overall culture did not, and when there was disdain for the poor, Christians brought compassion and solidarity. With the emergence of Christianity, a different vision of a just society and life began to emerge. Speaking of Christians, Aristides of Athens wrote:

> They love one another. They do not neglect widows. Orphans they rescue from those who are cruel to them. Every one of them who has anything gives ungrudgingly to the one who has nothing. If they see a traveling stranger, they bring him under their roof. They rejoice over him as a real brother, for they do not call one another brothers after the flesh, but they know they are brothers in the Spirit and in God . . . If one of them sees that one of their poor must leave this world, he provides for his burial as well as he can. And if they hear that one of them is imprisoned or oppressed by their opponents for the sake of their Christ's name, all of them take care of all his needs. If possible, they set him free. If anyone among them is poor or comes into want while they themselves have nothing to spare, they fast two or three days for him. In this way they can supply the poor man with the food he needs.[15]

Caring for the poor was uncommon in the pagan ancient world. The Jewish tradition emphasized care for the poor and outcast, but it was with the rise of the Christian faith that society began to change in its care for the least.[16] Paul Veyne writes that

> paganism was aware of the poor man only in his most commonplace shape, that of the beggar encountered in the street . . . [It] had abandoned without much remorse the starving, the old and the sick. . . . All this changed with the coming of Christianity, in which almsgiving resulted from the new ethical religiosity. . . . Old people's homes, orphanages, hospitals and so on are institutions that appear only with the Christian epoch.[17]

15. Longenecker, *Remember the Poor*, 61–62.
16. Longenecker, *Remember the Poor*, 60–61.
17. Longenecker, *Remember the Poor*, 61.

The Judeo-Christian faith of the early Greco-Roman world began to place in sharp focus the needs of the poor, the outcast, and the stranger. Longenecker argues that the Apostle Paul's admonitions in both Gal 2:10 and Rom 12:13 draw attention and praise to the hospitality and care for the poor that these churches were to demonstrate, in contrast to the wider cultural tendencies. Paul urges early Christ-followers to unite around care for the poor, despite their differences.[18] Early Christians began to distinguish themselves from the wider culture, in part, by their care for those who were overlooked.

A Living Catechism: An Early Christian Understanding of Suffering and Mercy

Even more so than now, suffering was a normal but unpleasant part of everyday life for the young and growing church. Christians expected to suffer and did not see it as an anomaly or an interruption. With little medical care, no modern conveniences, harsh living environments, and an age of brutality and rampant injustice, suffering was commonplace. Individuals in society had little control over their lives. Christ-followers did not expect suffering to go away, and therefore understood that their task was to endure. Suffering was not to be avoided. This is so clearly seen in the many Christian martyrs of the early church, who embraced suffering for the sake of their faith in Christ. Jesus Christ in the Gospel of Mark[19] does not glorify suffering or self-sacrifice but initiates God's kingdom, eventually bringing the overcoming of suffering. Christ alleviated suffering for some and empowered others to do the same. For much of history, suffering was an unpleasant but expected part of being human. In contrast, Western culture today sees suffering as abnormal or an aberration.[20] Our culture today provides untold numbers of remedies to physical ailments and seems to be fixated on protecting and insulating. Understanding how the early church viewed suffering is part of learning how they cared for and responded to the suffering of others.

Justin Martyr (100–165) noted the distinction that Christ-followers live as "aliens" or sojourners in the land while also seeking the best for

18. Longenecker, *Remember the Poor*, 144–45, 274–75.

19. Mark 8:34 NIV: "Whoever wants to be my disciple must deny himself, take up his cross and follow me."

20. Levine and Blickenstaff, *Feminist Companion to Mark*, 30.

others in their respective places. While the author is unknown, the following is dated to the same period in what is called the Epistle to Diognetus:

> For Christians are not distinguished from other people by country, or language or custom. Nowhere do they live in cities of their own, or speak a strange dialect, or live life in a peculiar way . . . they live in their respective countries, but only as resident aliens; they participate in all things as citizens, and they endure all things as foreigners. Every foreign country is their homeland, and every homeland is foreign.[21]

Augustine of Hippo built on the above-mentioned Didache and created what he called a catechetical approach to Christian maturity, which was a lifelong process of growing, learning, and engaging the truths of the Christian story for the continual formation and transformation of individuals and communities. Furthermore, in "Catechesis, Mystagogy, and Pedagogy," Beverly Johnson-Miller and Benjamin Espinoza emphasize the spiritual formation component of Christian teaching and instruction and note that "Catechesis is the process of leading others to embrace and be embraced by the love of God."[22] Spiritual formation always has an external expression of the internal mystery of God's work in the Christian's life. For Augustine, formation in Christ's love is an inward experience that manifests itself outwardly in sharing and leading others to the loving embrace of God. Essentially, catechesis is to be lived out in everyday life as we manifest and extend the loving embrace of God. Augustine was chiefly concerned with the "golden thread" of the twofold love of God and love of neighbor. These were inseparable and present in all aspects of teaching presented to new converts in North Africa in the early fifth century. Catechesis for Augustine was not just about disseminating information but was also about the spiritual formation of the soul that unites one with the transforming love of God.[23] This transforming love of God always has an outward expression.

Further, for fourth-century Cyril, bishop of Jerusalem, the Christian faith journey originates in and leads into the mystery of God's infinite love. Cyril wrote five homilies that defined mystagogic catechesis as a life to be

21. From the Epistle to Diognetus; quoted in Kalantzis, *Caesar and the Lamb*, 86.

22. Johnson-Miller and Espinoza, "Catechesis, Mystagogy, and Pedagogy," 156–70.

23. Harmless, "Review of *Augustine of Hippo*," 611–12 (see Canning, *Instructing Beginners*, 77).

lived, not a doctrine to be defended or a theological aspiration. Christian love in action is about living out the practices of the faith.[24]

The "Man of God" hagiographical literature recounts stories of a deeply devout man who rejected his inherited wealth and took a vow of poverty. One version in particular, the *Life of the Man of God*, is different from other common ascetic stories. It held much weight and influence in the fifth-century church in the port city of Edessa, part of the Byzantine Empire. It drew attention to the ideal Christ-follower whom all should emulate. In this version, the devout man performs no miracles and is not especially ascetic or penitential. His one extolling virtue is that he lived a life in solidarity with the poor and the foreigner. As he was dying, he was taken to the hospital for ill foreigners and was buried among the paupers. Stories of the "Man of God" captivated the minds of Christians and inspired them to care for the poor as they were visible manifestations of Christ. It is also interesting to note that by the fifth century, there were hospitals for the poor and the stranger. Eventually, the stories of this man of God who cared for the poor became linked with the name of St. Alexius.[25]

Gregory of Nyssa (ca. 335–395) of Cappadocia, was the younger brother of Basil of Caesarea and was good friends with Gregory of Nazianzen (all known as the Cappadocian Fathers). In his homily, "As you did it to one of the least of these you did it to me," Nyssa urged Christians to see the sick and the hungry as ones sent by Christ and to put on the "yoke of love."[26] He likened teaching the faithful the rudiments of knowledge to a teacher instructing children in the essentials of writing and pronunciation. For him, abstinence is a spiritual state of mind that examines the soul's relationship with sin. A state of abstinence yields self-control regarding food, clothing, one's relationship with money, and more.[27] Abstaining from excess creates room for generosity of time, money, and possessions.

Nyssa goes on to implore Christians to "assist these people (the poor, the starving in the streets, those who have no home and food, the leper, the ill and outcast), you who practice abstinence. Be generous on behalf of your unfortunate brethren."[28] Their ability and desire to extend mercy is linked with their discipline and abstinence. Nyssa understood that Christians

24. Johnson-Miller and Espinoza, "Catechesis, Mystagogy, and Pedagogy," 156–70.

25. Doran, *Stewards of the Poor*, xii–6.

26. Oden, *And You Welcomed Me*, 58.

27. Holman, *Hungry Are Dying*, 194.

28. Holman, *Hungry Are Dying*, 195.

have something to learn from the poor, for "[t]he poor are stewards of our hope, doorkeepers of the kingdom, who open the door to the righteous and close it again to the unloving and misanthropists."[29] Since serving the poor and afflicted embodies serving Christ, Nyssa implores all who follow Christ to remember him as they serve, because the

> Lord of the angels, the king of celestial bliss, became man for you and put on this stinking and unclean flesh, with the soul thus enclosed, in order to effect a total cure of your ills by his touch . . . remember who you are and who you contemplate: a human person like yourself, whose basic nature is no different from your own . . . treat all therefore as one common reality.[30]

Not only should Christians serve the poor because they are like Christ, but Christians should serve out of obedience, and, in doing so, will reap a harvest of blessings.[31] For Nyssa, each human being is an image of God and this understanding of the *imago Dei* influenced his opposition to slavery, "a stand that made him unique and countercultural in his time."[32] To arouse believers' passions and compassion in giving aid to those who suffer, both Gregory of Nyssa and Gregory of Nazianzen describe in detail the different ailments and predicaments that may befall one who is destitute.[33]

Gregory of Nazianzus explains in Oration 14 how all virtues are admirable and praiseworthy, but the greatest is active love for victims of misfortune, for each human being bears God's image.[34] Practicing excess leads to a sickness of the soul and the only remedy is to "follow the Logos by learning temperance."[35] Practicing love for the neglected is a preventative treatment for the sickness of the soul. It is both mandatory for the Christian and in one's best interest because to minister to the leper is to minister to Christ himself. Humans need this remedy to the excesses of the soul.

The relationship between theology and social ethics in the form of poverty relief continued into the fourth century. The Cappadocian Fathers helped highlight the invisible poor by locating them within the sphere of God's creation. Holman describes their contribution: "Basil and the

29. Holman, *Hungry Are Dying*, 196.
30. Holman, *Hungry Are Dying*, 201.
31. Holman, *Hungry Are Dying*, 202.
32. Carr, "Gregory of Nyssa."
33. Tobon, "Normativity of Measure," 242.
34. Tobon, "Normativity of Measure," 245.
35. Tobon, "Normativity of Measure," 246.

Gregories give meaning to the poor by placing them within the liturgical concepts of emerging Christian culture."[36] Furthermore, John Chrysostom (ca. 347–407), the great preacher in Constantinople, posits that almsgiving is the remedy for healing sickly souls. Not only is there benefit to the poor in giving but it also benefits the giver and is a part of their spiritual healing. Almsgiving was a discipline necessary for healthy spirituality.[37]

Furthermore, Chrysostom urges Christians to embrace their identity as pilgrims or sojourners on their way to God's heavenly city. For him and early Christians, identifying as one without place or home contributed to the acceptance of sharing hospitality with the sojourner and caring for the destitute. For Chrysostom, the idea of hospitality is grounded in one's Christian identity. Teaching was for formation that yields faith in action. There was no division between private devotion to God and acts of social ministry.

Writings and teaching originating in the early church are replete with instruction on caring for the poor, the stranger, and the outcast, and sharing hospitality with others as if they are Christ himself.[38] For the early church, orthodoxy necessarily led to orthopraxy; there was no distinction between the two. To be a Christ-follower meant to share one's life in ministry in the kind of ways that Christ did while on this earth. Christians were found with orphans, the infirm, the outcast, the stranger, and the sinner, addressing suffering where possible, extending hospitality, and leading all to the hope and good news of God's redeeming love.

In Genesis we learn that God created humanity in the "image of God," the *imago Dei*. Christians took this seriously in the blossoming early church. They learned to see the face of Christ in the poor and the suffering, the orphan, the widow, and the sick. Because of the resurrection, they learned to not fear death in contrast to the self-preservation of their culture. They accepted that to be human is to get sick and die. Their preparation for suffering involved teachings on learning and growing in suffering and empowered them to go to the suffering. Like firefighters running into a burning building, Christians "ran" to the plague victims during two major plagues of the time.

36. Holman, *Hungry Are Dying*.

37. Bae, *John Chrysostom*.

38. For more, see Lenhart, "Catechetical Instruction in the Eastern Church," 81–105.

During the Cyprian Plague in the third century (which was the second major plague), St. Dionysius of Alexandria witnessed the pagan reaction to the plague:

> At the first onset of the disease, they pushed the sufferers away and fled from their dearest, throwing them into the roads before they were dead and treating unburied corpses as dirt, hoping thereby to avert the spread and contagion of the fatal disease; but do what they might, they found it difficult to escape.[39]

Conversely, Cyprian of Carthage noted Christians' different approach:

> Most of our brother Christians showed unbounded love and loyalty, never sparing themselves and thinking only of one another. Heedless of danger, they took charge of the sick, attending to their every need and ministering to them in Christ, and with them departed this life serenely happy; for they were infected by others with the disease, drawing on themselves the sickness of their neighbors and cheerfully accepting their pains. Many, in nursing and curing others, transferred their death to themselves and died in their stead.[40]

Julian the Apostate also noted that Christians' care for the poor, and their compassion and service, were recognized as part of the ascendancy of the church. He sought to encourage Roman pagans to service of the poor, to no avail.[41] Wherever there was suffering, where people were overlooked, despised, and discarded, Christians were there, serving others as if they were Christ. They beautifully modeled "For whoever wants to save their life will lose it, but whoever loses their life for me will find it" (Matt 16:25 NIV, Mark 8:34–9:1, Luke 9:23–27).

Kavin Rowe describes how suffering is an important component of thriving Christian communities, drawing inspiration from the early church's understanding of suffering. He also cautions against concluding that all suffering serves some larger Christian purpose.[42] For the early church, facing suffering and sharing hospitality yielded fullness of life, invigorating the lives of Christians in the first centuries.

39. Sunshine, "Church's Response to Pandemics Throughout History and the Lessons for Today."

40. Jipp and Pohl, *Saved by Faith and Hospitality*, 119.

41. Rowe, *Christianity's Surprise*, 35.

42. Rowe, "Suffering Is a Part of Thriving."

Middle Ages and Reformation

The church during the Middle Ages addressed suffering and care for those who suffer in multiple ways, as seen in part of the Catechism of the Catholic Church, *7 Spiritual, and 7 Corporal Works of Mercy.*[43] This and other writings of the mystics linked care for others with one's suffering. Images of the works of mercy were often depicted through art, some of the most well-known of which are Caravaggio's altarpiece in Naples and Master of Alkmaar's polyptych in Amsterdam.

Considered the last of the church fathers, Bernard of Clairvaux (1090–1153) wrote *The Love of God*, describing God's four degrees of deep and abiding love. In the first degree of love, he challenges that the only way to be able to love one's neighbors as ourselves with "absolute righteousness" is first to love God, the source of all goodness.[44] Clairvaux noted the connection between one's suffering and one's ability to love and comfort others' suffering as Christ did:

> The sound person feels not the sick one's pains, nor the well-fed the pangs of the hungry. It is fellow sufferers that readily feel compassion for the sick and the hungry . . . [y]ou will never have real mercy for the failings of another until you know and realize that you have the same failings in your soul.[45]

Moreover, Clairvaux attests that discipline of appetites (not just from food, but from excess) frees one to love one's neighbor more fully and to give to those in need, trusting that God's love will supply one with adequate love to share.[46]

Living during the plague of the Black Death, mystic Julian of Norwich (1342–1416) wrote about the suffering of Christ and how his suffering envelopes or cradles those who suffer. In *Revelations of Divine Love,* she focused on Christ's suffering, which was borne out of his great love for humanity. She wrote out of her own experience with suffering and the loss of loved ones. While she may not have urged others to alleviate the sufferings of others, she did urge solidarity with Christ in suffering.

43. *Catechism of the Catholic Church*, "7 Spiritual and 7 Corporal Works of Mercy," para. 2447.

44. Gaultiere, "Four Degrees of Love."

45. Sri, "Mercy Melts 'Hidden Sin.'"

46. Gaultiere, "Four Degrees of Love."

In her seminal work *Dialogue* in 1377–1378, Catherine of Siena wrote practical encouragement in a time of cultural and ecclesial chaos. She devoted her life to serving the poor and the sick, penning, "I have told you how every sin is done by means of your neighbors because it deprives them of your loving charity, and it is charity that gives life to all virtue. So that selfish love which deprives your neighbors of your charity and affection is the principle and foundation of all evil."[47] Neglecting to show mercy and charity to one's neighbor is seen as the root of depravity. Catherine urged others to serve the suffering, just as she practically demonstrated this devotion in her daily life of service extending mercy. Contemporaries, both Julian and Catherine urged Christ-followers to see the suffering of Christ as a sign of God's immense love for humanity.

In *Obligations of Mercy*, Thomas Aquinas exhorted that Christians are bound to their neighbors and thus their suffering. He defines mercy as a compassionate concern for those who suffer hardship or grievous loss that compels one to comfort the afflicted. Mercy or *misericordia* means "compassionate heart." Charity is a result of God's divine grace, a byproduct of God's work of love and grace in our lives. For Aquinas, loving God means loving that which God loves. Human beings who bear the image of God then are objects of charity. Charity, for Aquinas, must include love for all that God loves, and each human uniquely bears God's image. Loving one's neighbor is how one loves God. Conversely, when our neighbor suffers, because we love our neighbor, we also suffer.[48]

Luther wrote catechetical teachings based upon faith, hope, and love, which are expressed in love of God and love of others. The point of catechesis was holy living as a way of embodying the Christian life.[49] The spiritual life was to be demonstrated in daily life in interactions with others. Luther had a broad view of catechesis in which the spiritual life was embodied.[50] Johnson-Miller and Espinoza write that the "Reformers warned against catechesis becoming an exercise in rote memorization and examination to the detriment of genuine interaction with people and ideas."[51] It was a lifelong process of spiritual formation and sanctification. Orthopraxy, or right practice, was the broader goal for Christian education and teaching.

47. Catherine of Siena, *Dialogue*, 35.

48. Floyd, "Aquinas and the Obligations of Mercy," 449–71.

49. Atwood, "Catechism of the Bohemian Brethren," 91–117.

50. Johnson-Miller and Espinoza, "Catechesis, Mystagogy, and Pedagogy," 161.

51. Johnson-Miller and Espinoza, "Catechesis, Mystagogy, and Pedagogy," 160.

Modernity

The Protestant Reformation gave rise to critiques of the established Catholic Church. As newly formed Protestant churches organized and mobilized for ministry, preachers exhorted their congregants to care for the poor and the stranger. Charity and social religion were common terms for this type of outward engagement of the church in ministry with the world in need. In an address on the anniversary meeting of charity schools in London on June 5, 1718, pastors William Lupton and Joseph Downing based their encouragement to extend love and charity to the neighbor on the example laid out by the early church.[52] Humanity's primary aim is the glorification of God, and the subsequent aim, in service to the primary, is engaging in "positive duties of charity." They go on to cite that trees bearing bad fruit should be cut down as well as those trees that bear no fruit at all. Indifference to sharing charity and goodness with one's neighbor is as bad as a tree that bears bad fruit. Both the stagnant tree and the tree with bad fruit are to be cut down and thrown into the fire.[53] For these Protestants, charity and good works were part of glorifying God and the Christian witness.

Not long after Lupton and Downing's ministry, in the city of Oxford, England, churches dissenting from the Church of England were beginning to form. In 1780, Daniel Turner, a dissenting pastor, urged newly forming Baptist churches to put on charity, which he affirmed is more than just kindness to the poor. It is the love of God shed abroad in hearts, extending mercy and loving-kindness, prompting Christians to do the greatest good for society. "Christian Charity is infinitely more than mere good-nature of that benevolence . . . it is indeed, the sum of all religion—Christianity in Epitome."[54] Serving and ministering with the world in need and extending mercy and love to one's neighbor was an essential manifestation of God's love in these emerging, dissenting Baptist churches.

The abolitionist movement in both England and America was often led by Christians who grounded their opposition to slavery upon their faith and understanding of God. One of these writers was an early Baptist layperson, Susanna Watts of Leicester England, who wrote hymns, pamphlets, and a book in the late eighteenth century. She contributed to *The*

52. Lupton and Downing, *Necessity of Positive Duty*, 22.

53. Lupton and Downing, *Necessity of Positive Duty*, 17–19.

54. Turner, *Charity the Bond of Perfection*, 2–5.

Humming Bird,[55] an anti-slavery publication, mostly written by women. Although these women writers did not sign their writings, we know that Susanna Watts and Elizabeth Heyrick collaborated together to appeal to both women and men, on behalf of their Christian faith, to do everything in their power to stop the slave trade, end slavery, and promote freedom.[56] Phrases like "dare we to alledge that Divine mercy is only for the white man?"[57] and "the work of emancipating the Africans is, therefore, a Christian work"[58] are found throughout their work in *The Humming Bird.* In it, Watts describes her efforts for an immediate cessation of the slave trade (as opposed to a gradual abolition) as a divine campaign.[59]

In addition to her written work in pamphlets and in *The Humming Bird* on the immediate abolition of slavery, Watts also wrote about and campaigned on care for the poor and the elderly. These causes were based in her faith and appealed to the Christian to extend friendship with those on the margins of life, especially slaves. She appealed to classical, scriptural, and philosophical texts to make her case against slavery.[60] Both lay and pastoral Christians continued the tradition of the church's ministry to the poor and the neglected, seeking to share Christian charity in meaningful ways with society.

At times throughout history, the church has responded to crises of justice with courageous positions undergirded by strong theological teaching. The Barmen Confession was penned by the Confessing Church in Nazi Germany with the help of Karl Barth and was a response to how the church in Germany was aligning itself with the government and thus becoming complicit in its atrocities.[61] Although this confession is not a catechism in the traditional sense, it is a theological statement, a part of catechesis and meant to instruct the church. Dietrich Bonhoeffer[62] addressed the pervasive suffering that surrounded him in Nazi Germany by calling on Christians to

55. *Humming Bird; or, Morsels of Information, on the Subject of Slavery.*

56. James and Shuttleworth, "Susanna Watts and Elizabeth Heyrick." "Susanna Watts and Elizabeth Heyrick: Collaborative Campaigning in the Midlands, 1820–34," in Winckles and Rehbein, *Women's Literary Networks and Romanticism.*

57. *Humming Bird*, "Address to the Ladies of Great-Britain," 201.

58. *Humming Bird*, "Illegality of the Slave Trade."

59. James and Shuttleworth, "Susanna Watts and Elizabeth Heyrick."

60. James and Shuttleworth, "Susanna Watts and Elizabeth Heyrick."

61. Busch, *Barmen Theses Then and Now.*

62. For more on Bonhoeffer's view of Christian responsibility to the state, see Bonhoeffer, "Church and the Jewish Question," 365.

stand with God in the hour of God's grieving for the poor and oppressed.[63] Both Barth and Bonhoeffer called the church to confront the suffering and injustices of their time. Some, like Craig Nessan, have critiqued the Barmen Declaration for being "myopic" and failing to intercede for oppressed and suffering neighbors[64] by focusing too much on the church's own welfare to the detriment of the welfare of neighbors. Bonhoeffer boldly proclaimed that Christians should advocate for just laws, give aid to victims of government injustice, and exercise civil disobedience when legal channels fail.[65] For Nessan, the Barmen Declaration did not go far enough.

Similarly, the Belhar Confession was forged in the time of apartheid in South Africa as a theological statement to guide and challenge the church.[66] Structured like the Barmen Declaration, it has three main components: unity, reconciliation and justice with biblical affirmation and a rejection of false teaching, stating, "any teaching which attempts to legitimate such forced separation by appeal to the gospel, and is not prepared to venture on the road of obedience and reconciliation, but rather, out of prejudice, fear, selfishness and unbelief, denies in advance the reconciling power of the gospel, must be considered ideology and false doctrine."[67] This is another example of the church responding to crises of justice by correcting bad theology that had contributed to complicity in racism. It demonstrates how confessional affirmations can arise from social ethics and social situations.

Today, some have called for the church to consider a new declaration to address the many societal injustices and to spur her to action.[68] Theologian James Cone, pastor Martin Luther King Jr., and activist Fannie Lou Hamer were among many Black Christians who prophetically called the church in America to repentance and into solidarity with the suffering of African Americans. Saint Oscar Romero and Pope Francis have challenged the worldwide church through their own work and writings to address the needs of the suffering[69] and to stand in solidarity and advocacy with im-

63. MacMaster, "Standing Where God Stands," 273–94.

64. Nessan, "Barmen Confession."

65. Nessan, "Barmen Confession." See also Bonhoeffer, "Church and the Jewish Question."

66. Huffel, "Belhar Confession."

67. The Belhar Confession, p. 7. https://www.pcusa.org/site_media/media/uploads/theologyandworship/pdfs/the_belhar_confession-rogers.pdf.

68. Shoemaker, "Does the Church Need."

69. Other current resources about suffering include Kilby and Davies, *Suffering and*

migrants and refugees. While there is no new theological declaration for the twenty-first century that addresses the social challenges and theological deficits of our era, there are voices speaking into the challenges of church and culture.

Dorothy Day, co-founder of the Catholic Worker movement, exemplified "hallowing" of bare life by paying intense attention to the suffering poor. The Catholic Worker movement stresses gentle personalism (the idea that every person is unique and has intrinsic value),[70] establishing hospitality houses for relief for those in need. Day's journals and writings chronicled the mundane challenges of community life in the hospitality houses and in the ministry. Understanding that each person bears the image of Christ was a foundational principal for her, as this journal entry from December 1945 notes:

> If we hadn't got Christ's own words for it, it would seem raving lunacy to believe that if I offer a bed and food and hospitality to some man or woman or child, I am replaying the part of Lazarus or Martha or Mary, and that my guest is Christ. There is nothing to show it, perhaps. There are no halos already glowing around their heads—at least none that human eyes can see. It is not likely that I shall be vouchsafed the vision of Elizabeth of Hungary, who put the leper in her bed and later, going to tend him, saw no long the leper's stricken face, but the face of Christ. The part of a Peter Clever, who gave a stricken Negro his bed and slept on the floor at his side, is more likely to be ours. For Peter Clever never saw anything with his bodily eyes except the exhausted black faces of the Negroes, he had only faith in Christ's own words that these people were Christ. And when on one occasion the Negroes he had induced to help him ran from the room, panic-stricken before the disgusting sight of some sickness, he was astonished. "You musn't go," he said, and you can still hear his surprise that anyone could forget such a truth: "You mustn't leave him—it is Christ."[71]

Throughout the history of the church, there has been a nearly constant presence of dedicated church leaders who have sought to model and teach the importance of extending mercy and justice to the suffering. Church

---

the Christian Life, and many books by John Swinton on faith, suffering, mental illness, dementia, and theology.

70. For more information, see Sisters of the Road, "Mission and Philosophies."

71. Ellsberg, *Dorothy Day*, 95.

leaders have done this through writing and teaching, through preaching and exhortation, and through their very lived examples of selflessness and service to the overlooked and forgotten—this is what we might call a "living catechism."

Examples of Hospitality and Mercy and Justice

In many ways throughout history, Christians have led society by tending to the sick, poor, orphans, widows, and sojourners by establishing hospitals and orphanages and by opening their homes to those without a place to stay. Monasteries and convents have always been places of refuge and safety for the vulnerable. Most recently in the twentieth century during World War II, many European convents and monasteries hid Jews from the Nazi regime. The Huguenot village of Le Chambón in France also offered sacrificial hospitality and refuge. Their risky and bold practice of selflessness was directly tied not only to their faith but also to their experience with suffering and persecution. They were acquainted with suffering and thus had compassion for the suffering.[72]

The underground railroad in America during the era of slavery was largely run by Christian abolitionists who risked their lives and families to help African American slaves escape to freedom. Today, hospitality houses can encompass many expressions and can be found across the nation and world as places where pilgrims can find rest and safety. Some hospitality houses offer a free place to stay while loved ones seek treatments in a hospital or a place of respite for those visiting the incarcerated. Hospitality homes can provide for adults with disabilities or teen mothers or serve as halfway houses for those in recovery. Catholic Worker houses[73] have long had footprints in communities bringing light and hope in forgotten neighborhoods. Hospitality or welcome houses help refugees and immigrants adjust to life in America, often providing short-term housing. Catholic Charities Immigration and Refugee Services and Lutheran Refugee Services often work with welcome houses as they support refugees during resettlement. All of these are examples of hospitality providing refuge for a vulnerable population.

72. See Haillie, *Lest Innocent Blood Be Shed.*

73. For more information, see Catholic Worker Movement, "About the Catholic Worker Movement."

Anna Rowlands cites inspiration from Simone Weil and Pope Francis as she exhorts Christians to see suffering and stare it in the face. She challenges others to pay extreme attention to the suffering and to attend to the material world instead of retreating and pulling away from the difficult parts of being human. Rowlands describes prioritizing being with immigrants rather than doing for them and creating a community of mutuality and reciprocity with refugees in a way that re-dignifies.[74] Throughout the history of the church, Christians have faithfully shared hospitality and mercy as an essential component of following Christ. We must resist the temptation to look the other way, but instead cast our gaze upon the suffering and let the Holy Spirit lead us in reclaiming hospitality as a faithful spiritual discipline for the twenty-first century.

74. Rowlands, "What Is Mercy?"

3

Equipping the Congregation

THIS SECTION ADDRESSES THE preparation of a congregation in the discernment of starting a hospitality house. Following is a proposed biblical study and overview of immigration and hospitality throughout the Bible that concludes with a section on current events and resources. This is an outline of a basic study a congregation might use. Through this study, Christians will see what Pohl asserts: "[h]ospitality is not optional for Christians . . . it is a necessary practice in the community of faith."[1]

An in-depth Bible study is already available on this issue in *The Bible and Borders* by M. Daniel Carroll R. This study draws on some of his work and addresses questions such as the following: "What is the biblical view of hospitality?" "What can we learn from Scripture and the early church about the 'stranger' among us?" and "How can we prepare for ministry with immigrants?" There are over 100 texts in the Old and New Testaments that address outsiders, immigrants, and the stranger or sojourner. There are at least twenty-four specific texts on welcoming the stranger and fifty-eight passages more broadly on justice and mercy. The Bible has a lot to say about how we treat the most vulnerable among us in direct admonition and through narrative story, as you will see below. This is an overview that can be tailored to fit specific congregational contexts and needs.

1. Pohl, *Making Room*, 31.

EDUCATIONAL PREPARATION FOR THE LOCAL CHURCH

A Congregational Study Outline

Below is a suggested outline that a congregation can use to develop their own programming to address the needs of their particular context. Possible discussion questions are included in the appendix.

Key Questions for Proposed Study:

- What is the biblical view of hospitality?
- What can we learn from Scripture and the early church about the "stranger"?
- What is our vocation/calling as the people of God?
- How can we prepare for ministry with immigrants?

Overview/Outline of a Proposed Study

1) Viewing the Old Testament through the lens of migration

    Week 1:

        Sarai and Abram and messengers, sojourner in Old Testament

        Levitical codes, Prophets

    Week 2:

        Exile in Egypt, wandering and return

        Displaced people, God accompanied/guided refugees

    Week 3:

        Ruth and Naomi

2) The New Testament and hospitality

    Week 4:

        Emmaus, Matthew 25, Paul, Jesus

        1 Peter written to those in exile, displaced

        Sojourner in New Testament

Week 5:

Mary as the ultimate act of hospitality

3) Early church and church history

Week 6:

Understanding outsider and sojourner; justice and mercy

4) The current situation

Week 7:

Who are our mission partners? These are partners I have worked with but there are certainly plenty more: Cooperative Baptist Fellowship Immigration Advocacy, Faith Works, Lutheran Refuge Services, Catholic Charities, World Relief

How are churches responding to immigration?

Ex. Short-term shelters, food, clothing, opening homes

Week 8:

Why are people fleeing Central America and other areas?

What is the role of US policy in recent immigration and destabilization of the region?

5) Compile a team to develop resources for future training

Compile trauma-informed care resources

Compile a resource guide & asset map

Determine other models to learn from

For many of the sections above, there are beautiful images of art and music that can creatively illustrate the biblical passages and engage the learner on different levels. One way to frame this study is within the context of caring for God's creation. Liturgical churches that follow the church calendar observe a Season of Creation in the autumn,[2] which leads congregations to consider how they steward and care for all of God's creation. This proposed study moves beyond caring for the material earth to all that God has created, including our fellow humans. Our church observes a Season of Justice and Peace bookended by Juneteenth and July 4. These dates in the national calendar provide opportunities to explore peace and justice and

2. See https://seasonofcreation.org/.

that which has been denied, specifically regarding race, which makes it a good time to engage this study.

Viewing the Old Testament Through the Lens of Migration

Issues related to migration play prominent roles in such biblical books as Genesis, Leviticus, Joshua, Judges, Isaiah, the Psalms, Jeremiah, Ezekiel, Ezra-Nehemiah, Esther, Ruth, Acts, and 1 Peter. The issue of migration figures prominently in the Bible, occurring in every genre from Torah to the Epistles.[3] This study presents an overview of both Scripture and migration; any one of the texts could be used for a deeper dive that would be instructive and illuminating.

The people of God have a long history of meeting God in the foreigner and being the foreigner who needs help from God. Sarai and Abram entertained sojourners who were messengers in Gen 18:1–15. Their hospitality to these strangers yielded a surprising revelation from God and a blessing. Because of famine, the people of God were settlers who became slaves in the land of Egypt, enduring hardship, genocide, and oppression. The story of God's people wandering in the desert, fleeing an oppressive regime, is central to the entire biblical story. In today's era of modern migration to the southern border of the US, it is strikingly similar that migrants cross the desert fleeing violence, seeking freedom. In the story of God liberating the Israelites, God accompanies them on their journey as a pillar of cloud by day and fire by night. Both in Scripture and in our current situation of migration, we understand God as one who companions those suffering, including the asylum seeker and all who seek safety and refuge in a new land.

Throughout Exodus, Leviticus, and Deuteronomy (Exod 10:17–21, Deut 10:19, and Lev 19:18), God reminds God's people to extend care and hospitality to those who have little and to the foreigner, reminding them that they once were foreigners and sojourners.[4] Later, after being settled in their land for hundreds of years, displacement hits the people of God again, as they are forced to flee in exile from their own land and live in a new country under the rule of foreign kings. This Babylonian captivity lasted almost 60 years and is described in the book of Jeremiah. The identity of the Old Testament people of God is often one of a sojourner—seeking place

3. Rowlands, "On the Promise and the Limits of Politics," 70.

4. Lev 25:23 NIV: "you reside in my land as foreigners and strangers."

and stability, fleeing oppression, and living under oppression. Through it all, God is with them, challenging them, calling them back, and accompanying them in grief and in their journey.

In Scripture, God is depicted as the divine host,[5] providing manna and quail in the wilderness and setting a table in Ps 23, culminating with God's banqueting table in Rev 19:7. The prophets have much to say about justice and how society treats the poor. Isaiah proclaims the year of the Lord's favor in Isa 61, the same passage that Jesus read to inaugurate his ministry (see also Isa 58:6–10, 1:16–17, Jer 22:3). The kind of fast that God desires, is not one of abstaining from food but one of seeking justice by providing food for the hungry and shelter for those who wander. The prophet Isaiah describes that this type of justice-seeking is pleasing to God. Isaiah 61 refers to the Jubilee year and Lev 25, which is designed to keep Israelites from falling into debt and servitude which would place them at risk for becoming migrants themselves. The Jubilee year restores family land and forgives debt, equalizing the haves and haves-not.

The wisdom literature of Psalms, Proverbs, and Ecclesiastes extoll the virtue of seeking justice for the oppressed (Ps 10:17, 82:3–4, 103:6, 140:12, 146:5–9, Prov 21:3). These passages urge the people of God to pay attention to the poor and the oppressed as a central part of what it means to live a life of worshiping God. The Old Testament clearly instructs on the subject of foreigners or aliens in Leviticus[6] in not depriving justice in Deuteronomy[7] and not oppressing the alien in Ezekiel.[8] Zechariah[9] exhorts God's people to show kindness and mercy and Malachi warns against pushing aside the alien.[10] For each of these passages from the Old Testament, a leader or

5. See again Lev 25:23 where God is the host of the land, the people of God are strangers and foreigners.

6. Lev 19:33–34 NRSVUE: "When an alien resides with you in your land, you shall not oppress the alien. The alien who resides with you shall be to you as the citizen among you; you shall love the alien as yourself, for you were aliens in the land of Egypt: I am the Lord your God."

7. Deut 24:17 NRSVUE: "You shall not deprive a resident alien or an orphan of justice," see also 27:19.

8. Ezek 22:29 NRSVUE: "The people of the land have practiced extortion and committed robbery; they have oppressed the poor and needy and have extorted from the alien without redress."

9. Zech 7:9–10 NRSVUE: "Thus says the Lord of hosts: Render true judgments, show kindness and mercy to one another; do not oppress the widow, the orphan, the alien, or the poor; and do not devise evil in your hearts against one another."

10. Mal 3:5 NRSVUE: "I will be swift to bear witness against the sorcerers, against the

teacher could spend weeks of study to help congregants identify with the sojourner and with God's call of care for the oppressed. As demonstrated, texts related to migration occur in the Law, the Prophets, and in wisdom literature showing God's heart for the marginalized. The theme of hospitality runs throughout the Old Testament, which continues without interruption in the New Testament.

The New Testament and Hospitality

Building upon the identity of sojourner and pilgrim from the Old Testament, the Gospels present Jesus and the holy family as a continuation of this motif. Joseph and Mary must sojourn to Bethlehem to please the empire and search for shelter as pregnant Mary gives birth. Our Christmas carol "Away in a Manger" reminds us of this story, "no room for a bed." After the birth of Christ, the family must flee violence in the middle of the night for their safety, seeking refuge in Egypt. Many of the asylum seekers coming to our border also have fled in the middle of the night with nothing more than the clothes in their backpacks. In seeing Jesus as the divine migrant, God chooses to identify with all of those who seek refuge, fleeing violence (Matt 2:13–18). After Herod's death, they wanted to return to Bethlehem, but Archelaus was in charge and it was still not safe, so they went north to Galilee (Matt 2:21–23).

Not only does the Holy Family exemplify and continue the motif of immigrant and sojourner, but Mary, the mother of Jesus, typifies the ultimate act of hospitality. Upon learning that she was carrying the son of God in her womb, she replied, "Let it be to me according to your word" (Luke 1:38 NRSV). She embodied hospitality by opening her heart and giving of her life and body for the work of the Lord. She embodied *kenosis*, a pouring out of herself, a relinquishment of power, control and will in service to God. Her act of submission to the will of God by hosting the Holy baby within her body is the greatest example of hospitality among humanity. Because of Mary's hospitality, of saying yes to God—sacrificially hosting God, she was the first to learn and understand the meaning of Jesus and his life. Mary, exemplifying Simone Weil's practice of paying deep attention,[11] contemplates

adulterers, against those who swear falsely, against those who oppress the hired workers in their wages, the widow, and the orphan, against those who thrust aside the alien, and do not fear me, says the Lord of hosts."

11. Rowlands, "Politics of the Common Good," 70.

the work of God in her life.[12] Mary's open hospitality to the Almighty God led to hosting the Christ child and to Mary's deep contemplation on the love of God that she experienced. In her deep attention to God, Mary recognizes God as the hope for all who suffer, as expressed in the Magnificat.[13]

John 1:14 (NRSV) says, "the Word became flesh and lived among us," meaning God pitched his tent with us, referencing the days of Israel's wandering in the wilderness. In both Matt 8:20 and Luke 9:58, Jesus said the "Son of man has nowhere to lay his head" (NRSV), reinforcing Jesus as the divine migrant who sojourns with us. Not only did he journey with us, but per the Isa 61:1 prophecy that he fulfilled, he specifically came for the population of the oppressed and brokenhearted. In Matt 11:3–5, the climax is Jesus's response to the disciple of John the Baptist that good news is preached to the poor. It is even more important than the dead being raised, also echoing Isa 61. Jesus is at the beginning of his ministry and foretells what the focus of his ministry will be: good news for the poor. Similarly in Luke 4:16–30 Jesus reads from the scroll of Isaiah and proclaims the year of the Lord's welcome, preaching good news to the poor, freedom for prisoners, sight to the blind, the oppressed are set free, and the year of God's favor, highlighting his concern for those on the margins of society.

Throughout the Gospels, Jesus seeks out those who are on the margins of life, the outcast woman,[14] the sick and the lame, and the despised tax collector, each time imparting dignity and sharing hospitality. Christ accompanies the brokenhearted on the road to Emmaus, and eyes are opened in the breaking of bread. Table fellowship and hospitality is a common theme that is also highlighted in the Last Supper. The disciples rely upon the hospitality of others as they teach and travel together, and the Lord's Supper becomes the great equalizing act of hospitality for the early church. First Peter is written to a congregation and people in exile, and the writer of Hebrews implores all to show hospitality to strangers, for by doing so, some have shown "hospitality to angels unawares" (Heb 13:2 NRSVUE).

The outsiders are the poor, the lame, the stranger, marginalized women and children, and even Samaritans and gentiles. The story of the good Samaritan[15] redefines neighbor and challenges the understanding

12. Luke 2:19 NIV: "Mary treasured up all these things and pondered them in her heart."

13. Luke 1:46–55.

14. John 4:1–42.

15. Luke 10:25–37.

of eternal life, which begins now with how we love God and treat our neighbor. No one is "not-neighbor," and Christ challenges all to go and be neighbors to others. In so many passages in the Gospels, the outsider is the one who understands what insiders cannot, reminding us that we have something to learn from the outsider. The Samaritan, an outsider, understood the core of the Gospel, to care for those in need, blind Bartimaeus sees,[16] children are brought close,[17] and the poor and those who mourn are blessed.[18]

Matthew 25:35–40 presents a story of judgment, "for I [the king] was hungry and you gave me food, I was thirsty and you gave me something to drink, I was a stranger and you welcomed me, I was naked and you gave me clothing, I was sick and you took care of me, I was in prison and you visited me." Jesus once again identifies himself as the outsider, the least of these. To neglect the vulnerable is to turn away God. In the story of Jesus and the Samaritan woman in John 4, he goes out of his way to be with a foreigner and outsider, one looked down upon and despised. It was shocking that Christ conversed with the Samaritan woman, who seems to have been an outsider, getting water alone; yet, in this divine encounter, people are changed. She was so astonished by her encounter with Christ, that she left her water jar and ran back to the town. Many followed her back to the well and met the Lord and believed. For Christ offered a water of a different sort.[19]

Christ's meals in the Gospels demonstrate God's hospitality as Christ embodies the role of *divine host*, offering a foretaste of God's kingdom where lives are transformed in hospitality and community. The repeated recipients of God's welcome are the poor, outcasts, and the marginalized. In the Gospel of Luke, Christ's ministry is the embodiment of God's welcome and Isaiah's exhortation to display hospitality,[20] sharing meals, and extending God's saving presence that yields transformation. This also appears in Luke 5:29 at the feast hosted by the tax collector, in Luke 7:36–50 with the Pharisee and sinful woman, and in Luke 14 Christ invites the poor, the lame, the crippled to the great banquet.[21] The parable of the great banquet reinforces God and Christ as the *divine host*. In the divine hospitality of

16. Mark 10:46–52.

17. Matt 19:14; Mark 10:14.

18. Matt 5.

19. Luke 4:1–42.

20. Isa 58:7 NRSVUE: "share your bread with hungry."

21. Luke 14:1–23.

God, Jesus Christ opened his heart to the world, ready to receive all who might come. These texts challenge us to consider how we, the church, receive the hospitality of Christ and in turn give it. Joshua Jipp, in *Saved by Faith and Hospitality*, writes that such experiences with Jesus as divine host result in a response: "Divine hospitality elicits human hospitality."[22]

Romans 12:13 encourages Christians to "contribute to the needs of the saints, extend hospitality to the stranger," equating strangers with the saints of God. Christ himself was a stranger and a foreigner, moving from town to town, continuing the motif of God on the move from the Old Testament. One cannot consider the theme of hospitality without considering all the times in which Christ broke bread and changed lives in the feedings of the masses, the Last Supper, and the meal in Emmaus. Jesus Christ's ultimate demonstration of hospitality are his outstretched arms on the cross, ready to receive all to himself. God as the divine migrant and the divine host are themes woven through Scripture.

The word "Christian" means Christ follower, one who follows in the path of Christ. The New Testament depicts Jesus as the divine sojourner and host; thus, we who follow Christ are to imitate these attributes. Philippians 3:20 reminds the church that our ultimate citizenship is in heaven and that we are strangers and foreigners in this world. Galatians 3:28 further breaks down any identity we otherwise might have, "there is neither Jew nor Gentile, slave nor free, male nor female; for you all are one in Christ Jesus." Our identity is to be that of Christ, the one who sojourned with us, sharing hospitality with the outsider.

In Galatians, Paul reminds the gentile Christians that circumcision is not necessary for being a Christ-follower, but remembering the poor is. This was a key part of the first church decisions in which the apostles decided what were the most important parts of the blossoming Christian movement.[23] What unites all Christian groups is their faith in Christ and that they remember the poor.

The Early Church and Church History

Since the entire first section of this book was devoted to how the church throughout time has engaged the culture in ministry with those who suffer,

22. Jipp, *Saved by Faith and Hospitality*, 177.

23. Acts 6 seeks to address the daily distribution of food to the poor and widows by establishing deacons.

I will not repeat the information. For a comprehensive congregational study, it will be helpful to address the rich tradition handed to us by the church. It is important to equip the congregation that ministry with asylum seekers stands on a strong foundation of the long history of the church and the people of God. Sometimes, churches neglect to teach church history because it is "not in the Bible," however it is important to show that serving and ministering to the suffering of the sojourner and the asylum seeker is something that Christians have done in the name of Christ throughout history. These chapters offer a wealth of information to draw on for teaching the history of the church's engagement with the poor.

The Current Situation for Asylum Seekers

Because there is so much misinformation in the media, especially about asylum seekers, it is critical that preparatory training and teaching cover the truth and the complexities of this legal and political dilemma. If possible, have someone visit with you who works in a reputable ministry on the border. Most denominations have missionaries and aid agencies on the border, and they will be the best resources. I can recommend the Cooperative Baptist Fellowship Immigration and Advocacy Team and field personnel in the Rio Grande Valley of Texas, Fellowship Southwest, Lutheran Refugee Services, World Relief, and Sister Norma and her work in south Texas,[24] just to name a few. Most of the big refugee resettlement organizations such as the World Council of Churches and International Rescue Committee also have helpful information and resources for churches. DASH (Dallas Fort Worth Asylum Seeker Housing) Network in Fort Worth Texas is a good resource for those in Texas, and Catholic Charities is doing a lot of good work for immigrants in the Rio Grande Valley and in the big cities of Texas. While it might be difficult to talk about the political and legal ramifications of immigration in church, it is very important to address misinformation which can easily prevent someone from fully engaging with the issue from a Christ-centered perspective. The National Immigration Forum advocates on Capitol Hill for immigration issues and has up-to-date information about bills under consideration. Each week, Adam Isacson with the Washington Office on Latin America (WOLA) offers information on the southern border, and in my experience is a good source for reputable updates and information. He highlights the often-difficult history between

24. O'Connell, "Sister Norma Pimental."

the US military and Latin America.[25] It is important to consider the US's responsibility and the role of US policy in the Latin American diaspora and destabilization of the region.[26]

Second, another crucial step is to learn from churches that are addressing the need and ministering with asylum seekers. Join weekly Zoom calls with organizations and churches working with asylum seekers across the country to learn what others are doing and how they are doing it. After hearing statistics and facts, seeing headlines and billboards, and reading the news, it is natural to feel helpless and hopeless. When this happens, a ministry or action never gets off the ground. Seeing firsthand what other congregations are doing is a crucial step in moving a congregation from contemplation into action. Once people see other normal, mid-size congregations doing amazing work in the name of Christ, the idea is de-mystified. It is strengthening to learn from others ministering in this way.

Mark 8: Following Christ

Finally, I conclude with a look at Mark 8:34 and Christ's call to discipleship. In all three Synoptic Gospels, Christ reminds his disciples what it means to follow him: "If anyone would come after me, let him deny himself and take up his cross and follow me" (Mark 8:34; see also Luke 9:23, Matt 16:24). For many in the North American church, our lives have become isolated from the "least of these" (Matt 25:40), which includes the poor, the outsider or stranger, the hungry, and the sick. A major challenge and area of growth for my congregation has been to step out of our insulated lives and into the more intentional ministry with the "least of these." When we are engaged with suffering persons in the world, we are living fully into whom God has called us to be as followers of Jesus Christ.

Anyone who seeks to follow Christ must deny themselves, take up their cross, and follow Christ. Who is this Christ we follow? As demonstrated throughout Scripture, he is a sojourner. He is always on the move, going to the suffering and those on the margins of society. Following Christ leads us into relationships with the same kind of people with whom Christ had relationships—the poor, the outcast, the sick and those who suffer. Christ exists in community as the Trinity, Father, Son, and Holy Spirit in a

25. https://adamisacson.com/.

26. For more information, see Washington Office on Latin America for more information: https://www.wola.org.

relationship of mutuality. What does it mean to follow Christ who lives and reigns in community? It means we, too, invest in community and give and receive in humility and mutuality. We walk with Christ as Christ companions and walks with us. When we look at the Christ of Scripture, we see that he walked, often out of his way, to be with the sick, the suffering, and the outcast. Fulfilling the prophecy as he read from the scroll of Isaiah,[27] Christ inaugurated his ministry, proclaiming that his ministry would be for the prisoners, the oppressed, the brokenhearted, and the infirm. As the body of the Christ, the church should continue this ministry today as we follow Christ.

What does it mean in Mark 8 to take up our cross and deny self? Denying self does not mean self-flagellation or starving ourselves. It means we let go of our wants and compulsions and put them in right relationship to God—putting God's purposes first. This does not mean that we are spiritually or emotionally unhealthy, or let other people abuse us, but it does mean that we yield our desires that are not aligned with what and whom God has called us to be. Mary, the mother of Jesus, is the ultimate example of letting go of our desires and seeking God's kingdom first, as demonstrated in her prayer, "Let it be unto me according to your word" (Luke 1:38). She demonstrated the epitome of hospitality by yielding her desires to that of God's plan and bearing in her body the Christ child. Her entire physicality was reoriented to God's ways and to God's calling upon her life, for the sake of the world. In much the same way, God's callings upon our lives will reorient us. It is consuming at times, and we bear the weight of it in our bodies and spirits. Mary's hospitality to God exemplifies this idea in Mark 8:34–35, that we are to deny ourselves, take up our cross, and follow Christ. As we open ourselves in hospitality to God, we follow Christ in ministry with the "least of these" (Matt 25:42–45).

Throughout the New Testament, the motif of God's care for the sojourner is embodied in the life of Christ who was a refugee. God chooses to identify Godself with those seeking refuge and asylum. Christ also embodies holy hospitality and divine welcome, and Jesus acts as divine host instituting the Eucharist. Jesus redefines neighbor, and Christ followers embrace their ultimate citizenship in heaven. These all make a compelling case for turning our gaze to the suffering and specifically to those seeking

27. Luke 4:17–21 from Isa 61:1–2 NRSVUE, "The Spirit of the Lord is on me, because he has anointed me to proclaim good news to the poor. He has sent me to proclaim freedom for the prisoners and recovery of sight for the blind, to set the oppressed free, to proclaim the year of the Lord's favor."

asylum. The call of God to care for the foreigner should ring louder than any negative press and misinformation. Politicians and lawmakers can debate the political and legal solutions, but Christians should never forget that God gives the church the responsibility to care, regardless of whether someone has the right papers, can speak English, or has come to the border the "right way."

4

The Nuts and Bolts of Developing a Ministry

After studying Scripture and church history, the hearts of the congregation and leaders are more ready to discern a calling. Having a clear vision or understanding of a calling to this type of ministry is important in creating plans. Unfortunately, there are no instructions for opening a hospitality house for asylum seekers, as each context is different. Getting some clarity about God's calling, however, will help shape the work of building this ministry. This chapter explores how to begin building a ministry of this sort, interspersed with excerpts from the journal I kept throughout the process. We begin first by addressing vocational calling and transformation, which aid in envisioning a ministry and setting the structure and boundaries for it using a strengths perspective.

Now that we have laid a strong foundation of biblical and ecclesial precedence for extending hospitality to asylum seekers and the church has accepted the challenge to reclaim hospitality as an essential practice for the church today, we can consider building a ministry. While some might suggest that their church has not engaged in hands-on ministry with those on the margins, like the asylum seeker, because they have not received a calling from God, I propose that it is quite difficult to receive a calling from God if the soil has not been tilled or fertilized or if the congregation or person is not primed or ready to hear. I never considered that I could possibly be a senior pastor in a congregation until I served on staff in a church that called a woman as the senior pastor. I knew that God had called me to ministry, but I had not seen a woman as a pastor and therefore my imagination could not envision being a pastor myself. Once I was on staff in a church that had a woman as a senior pastor, I could then begin to entertain the question, "Could I be called this?" "Am I being called to this?"

In the same way, the theological and biblical preparation of chapter 2 is essential in creating space for the Holy Spirit to go about the work of calling, molding, and shaping a church's vision and passion for ministry. Seeking to be who God has called them to be, Christ-followers must consider and ponder questions of calling and vocation. How do we create space for God to call us? How do we listen to God? What is our Christian vocation? What is the vocation of the church? What is your vocation and calling, as a child of God and as a local church, in particular? The study in the previous chapter is an essential part of the preparation for hearing and sensing God's guidance and calling.

VOCATION AND CALLING

Baptism is our basic ordination and a sign of God's call in our life. Stanley Hauerwas and Will Willimon in *Resident Aliens* assert that each Christ-follower has a mission in the world: "All Christians, by their baptism, are 'ordained' to share in Christ's work in the world."[1] Well-meaning Christians can get sidetracked from this vocation by any number of enticing avenues. Often, "good" things distract us from the best that God has for us, which can be participating in God's work and ministry in and around us. Work, family and recreation, all good gifts in and of themselves, can become the very things that prevent Christians from engaging in ministries like a hospitality house. To be honest, a ministry of sharing life does take emotional investment and time, which are rare commodities in our day and age. It may require rearranging our schedules and lives. Few Christians seem to take seriously that we are to share in Christ's work in the world: we are called to be co-laborers with Christ.

A notable exception to this age of distraction is highlighted in *Latina Evangélicas*, which systematically describes the pairing of social action and justice as essential expressions of the Christian faith for Latina theology. As a part of participating in God's reconciling work in the world, Elizabeth Conde-Frazier writes, that Latina "[w]omen have expanded the understanding of the mission of the church to include social justice or 'holistic ministry,'

1. Hauerwas and Willimon, *Resident Aliens*, 113.

meaning 'serving the spiritual and social needs of others."[2] Maybe it is their close proximity to suffering that has provided fertile ground for the Latina community to claim justice as an essential component of the Christian faith. The Anglo, North American church has a lot to learn from Latina theology and praxis.

In the previous chapters, we have seen how the early church interpreted this in ministry with the suffering and overlooked. We also looked at the biblical witness of caring for the sojourner and outsider and specifically at Christ's own ministry of healing and restoration with those who were hungry, sick, and outcast. In this chapter, we will address how our understanding of vocation impacts how we approach life and ministry. For our congregation, the calling was to accompany asylum seekers in ways that lead to life and Christian community. This calling guided how we structured our ministry, and this chapter is about that structure.

In *Resident Aliens*, Hauerwas and Willimon write of a pastor who stood up in a meeting of concerned citizens arguing against the desegregation of schools in the South. He was a pastor and an ordinary person who had labored long and hard, earning respect in the community and faithfully showing up in people's lives day in and day out. All of this prepared him for that night at the community meeting where he addressed an angry room and successfully persuaded the community to embrace the desegregation of schools. Living out our Christian vocation, which is necessarily ethical, simply boils down to "an ordinary person living out the Christian life before other ordinary people."[3] We have a Christian vocation to be God's people in our respective places, and sometimes we have specific callings to certain places or people. This is the intersection at which our congregation found ourselves—trying to discern God's particular calling and wondering if stepping out into the great unknown of opening a hospitality house was God's guidance and our work to do.

This journal entry describes my own calling as it unfolded, and that of our congregation, for this ministry of hospitality with asylum seekers:

> Vocation and calling are complex. We have a Christian vocation as a Christ-follower and congregations have a vocation to be the people of God in their respective locations. As Christians, our Christian vocation should overlap and inform our professional vocations. For example, in our work (as an educator or a farmer),

2. Conde-Frazier et al., *Latina Evangélicas,* 90–94.

3. Hauerwas and Willimon, *Resident Aliens*, 111.

we live out our Christian vocation to be a Christ-follower. As a minister my professional vocation is a part of a specific calling from God to be a minister. I count this as gift and blessing to have this call and intersection that many do not have. It is a privilege to have my work, my Christian vocation, and my calling all overlap completely. Many Christians sense a specific calling to a specific job or community as a part of their Christian vocation. At times, we can sense a particular call to a particular type of ministry, and this is what happened with the calling to start a hospitality house. It started so small because of little exposures to the needs of others. I believe it also grew because of our congregation's contemplative spiritual practices. In that deep listening and looking, God moved in multiple hearts at the same time. In so many ways, it has been a journey of transformation for all of us. At first, I truly wrestled with what I was beginning to discover as God's calling on me to help this process of a hospitality house unfold. I knew it would take so much energy from me, and I've wondered if I have had it to give. For a while I have told God, that I am not sure that I want this calling, as beautiful as it is. I have had to come to a place of deep surrender to the work of God. I find that I too often have to surrender again, for at times it feels like a roller coaster. I have experienced beautiful highs and deep and discouraging lows with this ministry. Ultimately, the certainty of God's leading has sustained me and the gifts of participating in beautiful God-moments have propelled me forward. My prayer life and the practice of lament have deepened in surprising ways.

Transformation

Stepping into the unknown of starting a hospitality house is an act of trust and hope that God still calls and moves in and among the people of God on behalf of the world. It is an act of faith, and it can be exciting as well as unnerving. There are unknowns and a lot of questions, and just as many who have gone before us were transformed when they said "yes" to the Holy Spirit's vocational calling. We can trust that we will be transformed along the way, too.

Two weeks before he was murdered while offering the bread and cup of the Eucharist, Archbishop Oscar Romero entered the cathedral in San Salvador to celebrate mass. He wrote about it in his diary saying:

> I went to celebrate Mass in the presence of the bodies of nine people killed by the military repression, which have been in the cathedral since yesterday. I used the message of the homily to say that those bodies are a lesson about the elevated destiny that human beings have—eternity. They are an indictment of the sin that rules on earth to such an extent that it can kill in this way.[4]

He presided as archbishop for a short period in the time of a reign of violence, during which his impact was amplified and far-reaching. His preaching centered around God's love for the poor and the Christian vocation of "conversion" as he put it—allowing God to transform us from the inside out so that we may in turn extend the hospitality of Christ.[5] This image of him preaching in the presence of martyred bodies exemplified his life, and he was canonized a saint in the Catholic Church in 2015.

When Romero received the position of archbishop three years earlier, no one foresaw that he would become the bold leader who stood with the poor, who spoke truth to power, who walked the streets and countryside of El Salvador listening to the cries of the brokenhearted and oppressed, and who stood among the dead offering the Eucharist. The story of Oscar Romero is one of transformation. Not the radical choice, he was chosen to lead because he seemed to be one who might not rock the boat.[6] He was the "safe" choice. As Romero submitted to the work that God called him to do, shepherding a people who were oppressed and terrorized, the seeds of internal transformation began to sprout in him. By opening his heart in hospitality to the sufferings of God's people, his heart also was changed. Walking, praying, listening, and preaching, he became the voice for the poor and oppressed of El Salvador.[7] His death was one among hundreds who lost their lives in ministry and service to God in El Salvador, including four women missionaries from the US murdered later that year.

Romero preached on the power of love and forgiveness while also calling for reform and justice for the poor. He encouraged those who had been wronged to take on the love of Christ and to extend forgiveness. Even if it meant disobeying orders, he called on perpetrators of violence to lay down their arms and follow the way of Christ. Romero showed us what the

4. Romero, *Scandal of Redemption*, 104.

5. Romero, *Scandal of Redemption*, 57.

6. Romero, *Through the Year with Oscar Romero*, xii.

7. To put his impact in perspective for North Americans, Oscar Romero is to El Salvador what Martin Luther King Jr. is to the US.

gospel looks like when lived out in love in the face of sin. Known for walking through the streets visiting with people and listening to their stories, he saw in each person the image of Christ. Just before his murder at the chapel altar, he preached: "Nothing is so important to the Church as the human person, above all, the person of the poor and the oppressed, who besides being human beings, are also divine beings, since Jesus said that whatever is done to them, he takes as done to him."[8] Any violence against another goes directly to the heart of God is an echo of what Jesus said in Matt 25, "whatever you have done to the least of these you have done to me."

The gift of Oscar Romero to us today, to the church squarely situated in North American privilege, may just be the courage to step forth into the vocational calling that Christ has for us and to allow that calling to transform us. Guided by his understanding of seeing the image of Christ in the other, he learned as he listened to the poor, and his heart was emboldened for justice. When we step out in faith, even small steps, in the direction of the Holy Spirit, we will be changed, and along the way so will others as well.

Christian practices and disciplines often give rise to new knowledge—a new way of knowing and experiencing God. In the early church, Gregory of Nyssa criticized others for only relying on theological ideas and ignoring Christian practices.[9] We come to know God better through the practices of the faith. We cannot neglect the daily practices that sustain our faith: Christian community, worship, prayer, and Scripture. In praying regularly, in submitting to and listening to God through Scripture and prayer, we grow and are changed. Elizabeth Newman describes hospitality as a Christian practice in which we also meet God. This is not sappy, sentimental hospitality but hospitality and worship that are inexorably linked as participation in God's own communion: "Hospitality is our participation in what God is doing."[10] It is time to reclaim hospitality as an essential spiritual practice for the church today.

Through this lens of Christian hospitality, we can better understand the encounter between Christ and two disciples on the road to Emmaus in Luke 24. They were confused and concerned as they processed their disappointment with the stranger walking with them. They had been seeing it all wrong[11] and could not recognize Christ. It was not until the risen Christ

8. Romero, *Violence of Love*, 216.

9. Newman, *Untamed Hospitality*, 21.

10. Newman, *Untamed Hospitality*, 60.

11. Wright, *Luke for Everyone*, 296.

took, blessed, broke, and gave the bread that their eyes were opened. The one they thought was a stranger was the Christ—the one who came bringing new life. In walking on the road with a stranger, listening and learning, their transformation began. In the very simple act of sharing a meal together, the ordinary became sacred, and they recognized God among them.

Similarly, in the one who is different from and unknown to us, we have opportunities to meet Christ in the "other." This is where and how a transformation of the heart takes place. We *need* this conversion, as our mentor Oscar Romero puts it. It will pull us out of our siloed worldview and into the presence of Christ the stranger. In gazing upon Christ (as encountered in the "other") we are changed. The vocational call to share and receive the hospitality of Christ also includes our sisters and brothers who have been calling out to the North American church seeking reprieve from systems of racism in our country. And it extends to the pilgrim church coming from Latin America and around the world, to our border and to our state. Our churches are positioned at the crossroads of these needs and voices, and now we can walk on the road with them and join them on the journey. When we open our hearts in hospitality and worship with those who are "strangers"—those we may not recognize, trusting that in doing so we will meet Christ the stranger—our eyes will be opened. Ministry with asylum seekers is a journey of transformation for leaders and the congregation. Seeking transformation is a necessary part of designing a ministry that seeks reciprocity where the lives of immigrants and congregations are changed by the work of the Holy Spirit.

Envisioning a Ministry

Beginning a ministry of opening a hospitality house for asylum seekers is a daunting endeavor, which underscores the importance of having a clear sense of God's guidance. In our congregation, we kept moving forward, seeking clarity and confirmation about what we thought we might be called to. Even as we moved forward, we wondered if we were sensing God's calling correctly. As we walked, trusted, and opened ourselves to God, we became increasingly more convinced that God was meeting us in it. Ironically, the more we heard concerns and hit road bumps, the clearer our calling became. Each challenge we faced caused us to think and evaluate what we were hoping for and how we were discerning the Holy Spirit's direction.

Instead of being discouraged by these unexpected road bumps, it was as if the Holy Spirit gave us determination and energy for the challenges ahead.

To begin a ministry of a hospitality house for asylum seekers, one of the first tasks is to be able to envision what it might look like and how a congregation might extend itself in this way. It is helpful to visit others who are doing similar work. Seek and study multiple models of ministry and identify a model that aligns best with your congregation's strengths, knowing that you will have to adjust to make it your own. Some churches have short-term shelters, others have a church member who opens their home, and other congregations offer a room in their church to an asylum-seeking family. There are many models, and it is important to find some examples of this kind of ministry in action and study them. Consider your strengths and weaknesses as you look for models. This same strengths-based approach is useful for so many aspects of developing and maintaining a hospitality ministry. You may not find a model that exactly fits what you can do and that is okay. No two ministries or congregations are exactly alike. Seek collaboration with others doing similar work in congregations and visit them. Learn from them. Talking with real people, with real jobs and families, in congregations with limited resources who are doing the work, demystifies the project. When you can see that you do not have to be a social worker or a mental health professional, or a congregation with a lot of money to embark on the journey of sharing hospitality in this way, the task becomes doable. As noted in the previous chapter, learning and educating are crucial steps in preparing a congregation to develop a vision for this kind of ministry.

Also mentioned earlier, Scripture and church history have laid a foundation for the church to see in the "other," the stranger or the outsider, the image of Christ. Seeing Christ in the stranger is a crucial part of developing a vision for ministry with asylum seekers. The journal entry below ironically captures the idea of seeing Christ in the stranger and how an "outsider" understood the *imago Dei*. As this story demonstrates, it is often complicated to live this out in practical ways.

> Winnie is a regular. She has come for years to the church seeking assistance, sometimes for rent, sometimes for laundry or a car payment or for electricity. We have taken her places and then felt like we were bamboozled. She came for months, claiming that she was pregnant with twins. She was pregnant with twins for about two years, and she always looked the same. When we have used up our benevolence budget for the month and we have nothing to give

her she can become very hostile. We have tried connecting her with resources and agencies in town and she doesn't seem mentally healthy enough to understand that they want to help her. Living lies is how she has made it in the world so far, hustling churches for money $20 here and $50 there. It must be a full-time job. She knows the kind of benevolence each church gives and when they give it. She comes and then will not leave until we give her a ride somewhere. Our hearts are compassionate and want desperately for Winnie to have a better life. She seems to want that too. But she is caught in a cycle of mental illness, poverty and trauma that seem too big for anyone to fix.

Our last interactions with her were concerning and we worried for her.

"You should really lock that door, ma'am, I could walk in and shoot ya," "Pastor you betta watch out." "Don't eva unlock that door an' answer it."

Part warning, part protection? We were never quite sure. We were out of benevolence money for the month, and we told her we had helped her 6 months in a row, and we needed to save next month's money for another who needed it. She was angry. She came back two days later, on a Sunday morning, and began asking church members for money in the parking lot as they walked into worship. She cornered the pastor and me right before worship. I told the pastor to go on and I would handle it as he had to preach. I talked with Winnie and reminded her of our position that we had discussed on Friday. She was upset and yelling at me in front of the church building as parishioners walked in. I felt for her and the desperation of her situation. We had had a long road with her and could not seem to move the needle in any helpful direction.

"How can you turn away someone who needs help?" "How in Jesus's name can you do that?" she exclaimed.

"Winnie, we are out of money from this fund this month and like we said on Friday, we need to save this for another family next month. You can check with Mission Waco this month for help"

"They won't help me no more! Them turned their backs on me. I'm gonna have these babies any day now and you won't help me."

"I'm sorry Winnie. I can imagine this is so hard." I question this decision and feel caught and am asking myself—Jesus will you just come and redeem us all? How would you have me respond?

Walking away yelling at me and to anyone who might hear:

"You just don't get it do ya? Jesus gonna come back as a black woman! I could be Jesus right now and you are turning me away! Turning me away! I could be Jesus! You just don't get it."

My heart broke. You are so right Winnie. So right.

Ministry with people can be messy, even when we have the best of intentions as this story with Winnie demonstrates. Winnie understood that Christ is often met in the stranger. Knowing this makes it doubly difficult to say no as one giving and extending hospitality. However, having clear boundaries and a clear purpose of what a ministry can and cannot do is essential in staying healthy for the long haul. Knowing strengths and limitations helps with establishing boundaries.

Employing a strengths-based approach, evaluate the strengths and limitations of the congregation and the community. What are the resources and talent base within the congregation? Are there teachers and healthcare workers in the congregation who might be able to help navigate the school and medical systems? Are there small business owners who can lend support to immigrants needing to find creative ways to make money? Starting out small with one family gave us the chance to listen and learn, to build relationships and trust in the community. This was essential and also allowed us to take stock of our strengths, assets, and weaknesses.

It is important to enter this type of work with a realistic view of what you can and cannot do. It is impossible to meet every need, and it is easy to become overwhelmed and to try to be all things to everyone. Trying to address every need and inequality can lead to a serious risk of burnout. Ministries that do not have boundaries often seem on the verge of collapse. Burnout can easily creep in if you are not clear about what you can say yes to and what you need to say no to. Churches and ministries with immigrants must be able today say no, which is a hard boundary to set with well-meaning ministers and lay persons.

The second step in getting started is to start out small, which is one of the best ways to maintain boundaries and get a good feel for the strengths and weaknesses of the congregation and community. Begin looking for the immigrant community in your own town by helping teach an English as a second language class at a local church or some other organization. Connect, volunteer, and partner with organizations such as Christian Women's Job Corp, Church World Services, World Relief and Lutheran Immigration Services, or other non-profits in your town that service women and families who are struggling. Learn about and volunteer with the Headstart programs in your area and the local food pantries. Start small by developing relationships with those seeking asylum and learn from them about their needs and challenges. Build partnerships with others in the community doing similar work. Note the gaps in care and areas that the church might be able to address. What unique services and supports does the community have? Is there a bus system or a community college? Research and connect with the community. Many start nonprofits in our community only to find out later that other organizations are doing the same work. Duplication of services is not a helpful way to begin and not helpful for long-term sustainability. Develop relationships with partner organizations and begin building coalitions. Who in the community helps with housing and grassroots community development? Habitat for Humanity can be a good partner, along with immigration advocacy groups, the Hispanic Chamber of Commerce, and immigration lawyers and legal clinics.

Developing a vision, starting small, and building coalitions are necessary steps in developing a hospitality ministry with asylum seekers. Dream together as a team of church members, praying that God will guide you in accompanying the asylee. It is a process of discernment and development, of defining visions and refining dreams. Flexibility and persistence are signposts on this journey; they will be best friends that leaders must lean on over and over. Embarking on the process of envisioning and discerning can be complicated and feel like a roller coaster. As challenges arise, make space to creatively look at problems and seek new resolutions. There are good resources centered around discernment on a group and congregational level.[12] Avail yourself of these formational tools and stick close to spiritual formation practices as you go through the process.[13]

Denominational entities and sister churches can become significant partners with endeavors such as this. Do not be dismayed, however, if no other church commits to being a full partner. Remember, people often need to see it first before they can envision it and commit to it. As the Holy Spirit births a vision and passion in the congregation, the church or ministry team may have to lead out in it first, and trust that God will provide resources, people, and support along the way. Building strong community relationships and coalitions will bear fruit long after the ministry has begun and may very well yield future ministry partners. We were challenged early on

12. See Barton, *Discerning God's Will Together* and Benner, *Opening to God.*

13. Doughty and Thompson, *Companions in Christ.* Bill, *Sacred Compass* highlights the Quaker Clearness Committee process of group discernment. Fryling, *Seeking God Together* describes the process of group spiritual direction which can be helpful in discernment. Susan Beaumont in *How to Lead When You Don't Know Where You Are Going,* has a chapter on deepening group discernment during times of high anxiety and uncertainty.

to make all that we do replicable and to invite others to join us in the work at every step of the way. That advice has proven valuable and prophetic. Several other churches have been learning from us and are in the process of starting their own ministries of hospitality. This is hard but rewarding ministerial work, and having partners is crucial. It takes forethought to be invitational and collaborative throughout the process, but it is worth it. In summary, to begin, it is important to develop a vision, to start out small, and build coalitions and partnerships.

FRAMING AND SETTING THE STRUCTURE

This section speaks to "how we did it"—how we went about "building" the Naomi House as a hospitality ministry of our church. The following journal entry is from the early days of the process:

> On the first night that our larger team of church members met, the 25 gathered and spent time in prayer, listening as Ruth 1:16–18 was read aloud, as lectio divina. We reflected together on Ruth and on Naomi, and on the relationship that had been forged between them on that journey. We explored how both Ruth and Naomi are heroines in this story and in the midst of their collective trauma and grief they both stepped out in faith. I am struck by how similar this ancient story is, to so many experiences today of those seeking refuge and asylum. There is famine and forced migration, disease and death in a foreign country and migration again to save their own lives and secure a future. It is the most basic of human desire: to secure a future for oneself and one's family and people have and will continue to go to great lengths to do that. More importantly, we considered its implications for our identity and our mission as DaySpring Baptist Church. Those verses shaped our thoughts and our vision of ministry.

People often speak of Ruth as a "sojourner" or an "alien," but technically that is incorrect. In all ancient Semitic languages, "sojourner" is only gendered as male.[14] Males can be a sojourner and have certain rights, but because Ruth and Naomi were women, they had little status and few rights. They were barely considered people and yet there was provision. The Bible has over 100 verses on caring for widows, orphans, and sojourners or strangers in a land.

14. Tucker, "Old Testament Through the Lens of Migration," presentation to DaySpring Baptist Church (October 21, 2021).

The contemporary connection is apparent. So many of those who come to the border are not considered sojourners in the most generous sense; they are barely considered people. Listen to the rhetoric surrounding immigrants at the border, especially those from Latin America.[15] Read the accounts of children ripped from their parents' arms and put in cages. Those who seek asylum have few rights and status and are without home, place, and position. Our congregation sought to provide a place that offers a different narrative, one that is rooted in and guided by the gospel. Here is an excerpt from another of our first communications to the congregation:

> In the text from Ruth 1, people tend to focus on Ruth's pledge to Naomi, but they often fail to give attention to Naomi's response: "When Naomi saw that she was determined to go with her, she said no more to her." Knowing full well that it might cost her something, both socially and financially, when it made no sense to take someone else in to feed or clothe, "Naomi saw that [Ruth] was determined," and she could say no more except to walk alongside her in the journey.
>
> With God's help, we believe that the Naomi House could become a place where people who have no status, who are barely seen as people, could find a home and community, and we believe that it could be the place where we as a church see that they are determined, and we choose to walk alongside them in the journey.[16]

Living out the gospel call to walk where and how Christ walked often leads in a different direction than that of the surrounding culture. It is nevertheless the way of life. The story of Ruth became a guiding light for our congregation as we began to think about how to structure and plan for further developing a ministry with those seeking asylum.

THE PROCESS

Many have asked what led up to our congregation having this first night of dreaming together, and my answer is always that many factors, situations, and prayers brought us to the point of beginning to dream together how the church might extend itself in ministry with immigrants. Several instigating situations brought the issue front and center. Our friend, fellow pastor, and

15. Posner, "Why the Biden Administration Needs."
16. Dennis Tucker, letter to the DaySpring congregation.

colleague, John Garland, wrote an article for *Christianity Today*[17] describing his church's (San Antonio Mennonite Church) work with asylum seekers. Just two and a half hours south of Waco, San Antonio Mennonite Church was amidst an overwhelming immigrant situation, especially during the height of the influx to the border during the Trump administration.[18] They were extending themselves in significant ways with an overwhelming need, and our congregants wanted to help. I arranged a trip for twenty members of the congregation to visit and help in any way we could. We realized how small this church was and how few resources they had, yet they were making a huge difference with their Mary and Martha House, a short-term shelter for women and children searching for safety and seeking asylum. While there, we cooked with the women in the home, heard their stories of fleeing violence, and heard of their amazing faith in God. We visited the shelter set up by the city and spent time in prayer. While we were there, someone from our team asked Pastor Garland, "Should we open a hospitality house?" His immediate response was, "Yes!" Then he took it back and followed up with a "No. You shouldn't open a hospitality house. It is just too hard and difficult. We do need a social worker though. Maybe you can help us make connections and raise some money for one." We dreamt and prayed about this, went home, and raised $25,000 for their church to hire a social worker. At a debriefing time back in Waco, we filled our pastor in on what we had experienced, and Pastor Garland's words, "No, you shouldn't, it's too hard" echoed in our minds. It was as if those words became a challenge.

Vision and Values

Shortly thereafter, Pastor Garland called and let us know that one of the young women in the home, whom we had met, needed a place to live. She was eighteen years old, had a newborn baby, and she did not know anyone in the US. Our hearts had been heavy with concern about the situation on the southern border, and we had already met this young lady in the home. Now the immigration crisis had a face and a familiar name. Seeing a church ministering in this way opened our imagination, and our interest piqued. We were beginning to see ourselves in ministry like this, whereas before the trip to San Antonio, it felt like a huge overwhelming challenge in which we did not know where to begin or how to engage.

17. Garland, "Fleeing North in the Full Armor of God."

18. TRAC Immigration, "Record Number of Asylum Cases in FY 2019."

I contacted the group of church members who had gone to San Antonio and those who were also interested, told them of this young woman's need for housing, and a family from the church stepped up and opened their home. The church committed to walk alongside them in this ministry, supporting them in whatever way they needed, from helping with transportation, to English tutors, babysitters, prayer partners, friendship, and many other ways. This family's courage to step out, with the church behind them, allowed the church to also step out in a small way with a new kind of relational ministry. This young woman and her child became a part of the congregation, her child was dedicated in worship, everyone bought her tamales, and four years later, she was living in the Naomi House helping to provide transportation to the guests and helping establish a weekly meal in the home.

Initially, a small team formed around this family and the young mother when she first came, supporting, encouraging, and learning how to help connect the mother and child with resources in the Waco community. After several years of encouraging this family, another team began to form that wanted to engage more fully in ministry with those seeking asylum. We determined that women seeking asylum are really at the bottom of the list of those who are the "least of these" as Christ describes in Matt 25. They are at risk for violence, exploitation, and trafficking, there is no help from the government or aid agencies, and they cannot work or support their families for months until their work permit is approved. We also continually experience in our Texas culture the antipathy and disdain toward them, and our hearts were drawn to extending the love and peace of Christ amidst this hardship. This small group began meeting for prayer and dreaming, and eventually became a steering committee, exploring the idea of how the congregation might further engage in ministry with the asylum seeker.

In addition to the trip to San Antonio where a church family had taken in a young woman and her child, the next precipitating factor that helped instigate this ministry was encouragement from a local congregation. Hope Fellowship, a local Mennonite house church, contacted us and asked if we might be interested in purchasing a church member's house to use as a hospitality house for immigrants. They had heard of our growing interest in ministry of this sort, and they committed to pray for and with us about this opportunity.

In meeting and consulting with other faith leaders, I was challenged to find a way to make this burgeoning ministry replicable, to create a model that other churches might imitate. Additionally, I wanted to keep this ministry directly tied to the DNA of the congregation. DaySpring Baptist Church was founded in 1993 by a core group who were burned out from church work. They intentionally set the tagline of the church as "sacred and simple" and named the road to the church Renewal Way. They affectionately called DaySpring "Last Stop Baptist Church" as it was the 79th Baptist church in Waco in 1993, and because it already was the last stop for people considering leaving Baptist life, or even the Christian faith altogether. Because it was founded by people exhausted from church work, it has maintained a low footprint and little structure and overhead. DaySpring began embracing the contemplative life early on, and the congregation became a place of renewal and healing for so many who found their way there. After twenty years, however, the congregation still had not found its footing in ministry in the community. One of my tasks as Minister for Community Life was to explore what that might look like. The church was ready for a ministry it could wrap its arms around, and my challenge was to help it reflect the personality and passion of the congregation. With encouragement from a partner church and a ready and primed congregation, the seeds of years of contemplative spirituality were now germinating.

Discernment

In the formation of this ministry of hospitality, the church and I worked hard to keep all this history of the church in mind. What are the essential values of your congregation? How can you keep that at the forefront of your planning? It has been essential that we find a way to craft a ministry that reflects the ethos and values of the church: DaySpring is a place of renewal and healing; we keep things simple so that we can focus on the sacred. When the Mennonite Church offered their community house for DaySpring to purchase, we had to take a long look at how it fit in with our values of simplicity. The house was big, and a loan was going to be an even bigger stretch. We then leaned more and more into the idea of starting small, seeking replication. Eventually, we made the hard decision not to pursue purchasing this house, which seemed perfect and in the exact neighborhood that we had chosen as the best place for this ministry. It was discouraging at first, because we realized that the financial investment would be too high, and the house might be too big for what we were beginning to think we wanted to do.

As indicated, many factors contributed to the process of opening a hospitality house for asylum seekers, and we identified five more factors on our journey of discernment toward action. First, the church had a strong foundation of missional engagement in Latin America. Over the years, there had been a couple of Latin Americans in the congregation who planted seeds of care and concern for Latin America. Second, many were ready for "something"—a "what's next for the congregation"—to address the lack of a cohesive missional engagement for the congregation. Third, two presenting experiences pushed the issue forward: the crisis on the border and our proximity to it, as we heard of it through friends in San Antonio, and a church family opening their home to the young asylum-seeking woman and her baby. The fourth factor that continued to help our discernment was the relationship we built with this young woman and her baby and her assimilation into the life of the church. Every Sunday, her presence reminded us of what the body of Christ is called to be. Fifth, the church had a high sense of vocational calling to be the hands and feet of Christ in ways that impact the community. This was due to the church's overall theological and educational teaching. Specifically, we held a series on immigration and offered a lot of teaching on race and the church's role in race relations in America.

The congregation was primed and ready to hear a calling from God. As a contemplative Baptist church, some have thought that the church was insular; "navel-gazing" is a word that I have heard. And while to some it might appear that way, true Christian contemplation must always have an outward expression. Church members had many ways in which they were living out their Christian vocation in the world individually. Many had a high sense of vocational call, meaning the work that they were doing each week in education or health care was something they felt called to because of their faith. The church, however, had not embraced a call collectively. This high sense of vocational call among church members could have been a constraint on those who were busy and exhausted. At the same time, it was an opportunity because they were in touch with their desires to live out their faith in ways that impacted the world. Some wondered when or if the church would find its missional call but hindsight has shown that in our prayer and waiting, the Holy Spirit was ready to meet us at the intersection of receptivity and opportunity.

Seed Money: Seeing the Possibility

After the leadership team declined to pursue purchasing the Mennonite house, they went back to the drawing board, all the while communicating with the congregation the vision and the adjustments that were being made. The steering team continued creating a vision for this ministry, researching other ministries and models, and considering the steps necessary to lead the congregation in this way. Late in 2021, a church member donated $15,000 to the congregation to be used in some way for ministry with immigrants. Until this point, so much of the planning and discussion was without any money in the church budget for this ministry. The steering committee challenged the congregation to match this and quickly the church had $44,000 as seed money for the new ministry. During this time, a church member began conversations with the staff about offering a home he owned for the church to rent for the hospitality house. He had done a significant amount of work on the house and the steering team began to seriously consider this possibility. We were all drawn to the idea that a church member wanted to partner with the church in this way to help start this ministry.

By March 2022, the steering team began preparing to present a vision for the ministry so that the church could vote on allocating funds raised and create a financial plan to launch the ministry. The purpose and vision for the ministry, and the financial plan were later approved by the congregation.

Ministry Purpose Statement and Covenant

We began with a vision or purpose statement and tried not to get too specific about the details as we started, to leave room for improvisation and flexibility for what was to unfold:

> DaySpring's Naomi House will center around a common life and faith, sharing hospitality with the immigrant through mutual support and empowerment in ways that catalyze the congregation in ministry and invigorate our faith.
>
> Community Covenant
> To receive one another as Christ in our midst;
> To treat one another with dignity and respect;
> To participate in and share together a common meal;
> To address conflict in a way that honors one another;

To respect the privacy and private space of individuals within the home;
To participate in the stewardship of the house;
To pray for one another.

After much debate about what and how we wanted to minister, we settled on the hospitality house being an extension of the ministry and witness of the congregation. For a congregation whose motto is "sacred and simple," starting a hospitality house for asylum seekers did not seem simple, and we were aware of the cost and burden we were undertaking. Some wondered if we should start a non-profit instead and let that entity bear the burden of directing and organizing a ministry of hospitality. There are merits to that approach, but in the end, we let two things guide us in our decision about how to go about this endeavor.

First, we relied upon our church's theme of simplicity and decided to start out small and let something grow and develop over time. It could turn into a non-profit someday. However, we wanted to guard against "farming out" the ministry of the church. We opted to see some of the challenges we had at the beginning, such as finding a house, to motivate us to keep our scope narrow, start small, and invite other churches along the way to join us in this work. We also reflected upon how extending hospitality in this way is the sum of the gospel: to share God's hospitable love in a way that leads to renewal and Christian transformation. Understanding "simple" to mean distilling faith to that which is essential, the hospitality house made this faith expression more congruent with the church's ethos.

Second, we leaned into our church's emphasis on community and being a place of rest. So many come to our church seeking spiritual healing and renewal. It is a part of who we are that we make space for this kind of renewal, and we want to extend that same renewal to those seeking asylum. We sought to create space for relationships to develop and for healing to happen. We clarified that we wanted this ministry of hospitality to be an outpouring of the church's mission and ministry, and sought to make this ministry a reflection of the DNA of the congregation.

Who and Why? Latina Asylum Seekers

In listening to other ministries and congregations involved in caring for immigrants, one thing became clear: the need was overwhelming, and many people were burned out. We took note of that, hoping to avoid that fate. Good leadership is often said to begin with the end in mind. Avoiding burnout became one of those goals that we planned for and hoped to address from the very beginning. As a team, our hearts were initially drawn to the Latina asylum seeker due to our proximity to the border (seven hours). We heard their stories of fleeing violence and came to see that, in many ways, it is the migrant church coming to our border for refuge and safety. In addition to our compassion and desire for justice for so many of those at our border, we also had much to learn from them about their faith in God through adversity and trials. We recognized that the Church, and our little congregation, need a fresh expression of the Christian faith that the migrant church-on-the-move had to offer. We believed that we would encounter Christ in the sojourner, and we have. We have kept our scope narrow: women and children who speak Spanish and who come seeking asylum.

Our town had some resources in Spanish but little for other languages, so we kept our focus narrowly on Latinas. Over time, however, as the immigration climate has changed and fewer are coming to the border, we have learned a lot, and we are adjusting. We are now considering how we might expand to other languages and cultures in the home. Women with children are vulnerable to exploitation and have a huge challenge with finding work and caring for their children. Someday, we may decide to open our doors to families with men, but in the beginning, we started small and stayed focused. We have had to say no many times to people who did not fit our scope and that is always hard to do. We want to be in this type of ministry for the long haul, so we keep the goals of being manageable and replicable in mind as we plan.

Hosts and Guests: Roles and Responsibilities

Dietrich Bonhoeffer's work *Life Together* has long been a guiding framework in our congregation. During his time of study, he made his way to America, but God placed such a burden on his heart for his home country, that he returned to Germany despite the dangers. It ultimately cost him his life. He is known for his phrase "cheap grace" that refers to grace without discipline and without repentance. The Christian life must be lived out in a Christian's interactions with others and the world and is entirely sustained by life of prayer within the Christian worshiping community. Bonhoeffer writes about the role of prayer in the Christian life, that it extends beyond words into the whole day so that "every word, every work, every labor of the Christian becomes a prayer."[19] For many in our church, his legacy has influenced our understanding of community and prayer.

We have often studied and tried to apply what it means to live life together as the body of Christ in this place, leaning upon Bonhoeffer's ideas of Christian community. We created this hospitality house with the idea that there would be hosts who lived in the home and who were the face of the church for the women and children in the home. Their role has been to set the tone for the home with rhythms of prayer and a community meal. They help create a home environment where the love of Christ is reflected in the home. Over time however, we have had to adapt and adjust that specific desire and goal. Currently, we have hired a very part time house coordinator who lives in the neighborhood, visits the home regularly, and leads house meals and meetings as well as coordinated some of the enrichment activities in the home. It has helped us to stick close to our overarching vision to accompany, in community, the asylum seeker, and that has allowed us to let go of ideas that are not working and embrace new ways to structure the ministry that might work better. It is a constant work in progress, and we will probably never feel like we have "arrived" having a "perfect" solution.

The House: Structuring the Ministry

As we connected with others in the community who were ministering with immigrants, we developed relationships and word began to spread that our church was seeking to minister in this way. When the option to purchase a house arose, none of the other entities seemed to have the bandwidth to consider how they might use a house for immigrants. They gave our congregation time to pray about and consider if we might want to purchase this house for use with immigrants. It was a big house with many bedrooms, and we became excited and energized by the idea of it full of women and children seeking asylum. We also could have several church members living in it, in hopes of creating a space of community and life together.

We sought financial partners and had some lined up. Eventually, however, we realized that the loan was going to be too costly and difficult to manage. We were tempted to be discouraged, but we knew that God was leading us. It was a lesson in trust and turning obstacles into opportunities. This situation allowed us the chance to clarify our vision and remember

19. Bonhoeffer, *Life Together*, 71.

our guiding principle of seeking simplicity amid this new endeavor. We began to look for a much smaller house that we could rent. We doubled down on our vision to start out small and seek a replicable model. When a church member revealed that they had a house in the neighborhood we were interested in (due to its proximity to resources and church members) and offered it as a place for the church to rent, we saw convergence and doors opening. We were drawn to the idea of a church member partnering with the church in this way and wanted to honor his desire of partnership. It has been the perfect home for the hospitality house.

During our year of exploration of this ministry, we formed a steering team to explore options, learn, pray, and engage the congregation in preparation for a hospitality house. This steering team held church-wide conversations, prayer meetings, Bible studies, and many meetings thinking through each aspect of the project. An important book to read as a team during this time of preparation was *When Helping Hurts: How to Alleviate Poverty Without Hurting the Poor and Yourself* by Steve Corbett and Brian Fikkert and their follow-up book: *Becoming Whole: Why the Opposite of Poverty is Not the American Dream.*[20] These books empower Christians to care and serve in culturally appropriate and dignifying ways and challenges North Americans to not impose our views of what is good and worthy onto those we serve. While I do not agree with every approach in these books, they are helpful starting places for discussion about our own North American, Anglo biases that can inhibit a fruitful cross-cultural poverty-alleviation ministry.

In our next phase, we moved into several layers of support with a small leadership team, a finance team, and a hospitality and support team. The leadership team of four set the direction for the ministry, working with the chaplain volunteers for the house (mainly seminary students), and the interns and hosts, providing direction and conflict management. The finance team worked on the budget, addressing financial needs as they arise, and looking for funding streams outside of the congregation. The hospitality and support team sought to meet the tangible needs of the home such as groceries, transportation, mowing, clothing, English conversation partners, and more. Over time these teams and positions have morphed and changed, reflecting the fluctuation of needs of the ministry.

Dividing tasks among different teams allowed teams to take a deep dive into a certain area to develop a knowledge base of that area. Our goal,

20. See also the small group study and video series, "When Helping Hurts."

for example, was to have a couple of people who really knew the educational options in town and how to navigate them, and another team that understood the food pantry options, and so on—this versus having the entire team well-versed in all the details. After three years of this ministry, we have now found social workers who can help us far more efficiently. We have continued to build strong and helpful relationships with community partners who continue to enhance and improve the ministry. We have not maintained all of these different teams, but they served a purpose and were helpful. As the ministry evolves and grows, we continue to explore different leadership structures and models for how to organize our shared ministry.

Trauma-Healing Congregation

One of the resources of our community and our congregation has been the influence of a university with a school of social work and a seminary. These same resources are also available virtually for anyone wanting to embark on endeavors such as this, so proximity does not have to be a constraint. Through these resources, we have been able to arrange for training of our laity in areas of trauma-informed care and ministry.[21] Any woman who would flee her country and embark on a two-thousand-mile journey, through dangerous territory, must be fleeing some type of trauma or extreme hardship. The arduous journey is also one of violence and trauma; immigrants are often retraumatized. We spent a lot of time educating ourselves on trauma and cultural humility so that we could create a ministry that would be a space for health and healing for all involved.

Trauma-informed care understands and considers the pervasive nature of trauma and promotes environments of healing and recovery, guarding against practices and services that might inadvertently re-traumatize.[22] Persons seeking to employ trauma-informed care in their interactions with asylum seekers are curious about what experiences or beliefs might lie behind the actions or interactions that they experience. What is going on inside someone who might lead them to act in this manner? Those seeking to support asylum seekers need to hold confidences when appropriate and seek to build trusting relationships. Their story is just that, their

21. Baylor University, "Trauma-Sensitive Congregations." See also Baylor University's research on trauma and faith, "Trauma." See also https://traumahealinginstitute.org/ and resources in the appendix.

22. Murphy, "Moving Beyond Trauma." Ko, "Promoting Culturally Competent."

story; it is theirs to tell and not anyone else's to tell. This can be a challenge when trying to share the plight of immigrants coming to America, and we recognized that we needed to navigate it gingerly. We learned that typical interactions must be viewed through the lens of trauma, such as how we share a hug or even the way we speak and converse. There are aggressive ways to speak and interact, which in our society might be seen more as direct but to those who have experienced trauma, it can be received as aggressive. Our body language and our verbal communication must express listening, receptivity, and non-judgment. Because so much of the violence in Latin America comes from the hands of men, we learned how important it is for male volunteers to be mindful of their posture, body language, and interactions, always seeking to show deference and humility.

We knew trauma-informed care would be a part of our ministry, but we were not quite sure how it would surface. The effects of trauma can be seen with ongoing headaches and stomachaches, depression and having a hard time getting out of bed, heightened emotions and an inability to remember all the new information. It could also be seen in strong and visceral reactions to a balloon popping or a fear of going outside and not being safe. Children can be seen as aggressive or hyperactive or "difficult" as they sort through their trauma feelings and reactions. Trauma cycles are hard to break and those who have endured trauma can sometimes inflict trauma on others. For parents stuck in trauma, parenting is especially difficult, and parents can often re-traumatize their children. Through trauma-informed care training, we are learning to spot these cycles, refer for professional and help and have more understanding when faced with difficult or unusual responses. We are learning that what we once thought might be "unusual" responses are not that unusual after all.

Strengths-Based Approach

A strengths-based approach to care builds upon a person's (or organization's) strengths, noting their resourcefulness and resiliency in difficult and adverse circumstances. Developed in the 1980s at the University of Kansas School of Social Welfare,[23] it is centered around supporting persons to set and accomplish their own goals (not someone else's goals). This focus on strengths helped our congregation to determine what we might be good at and where we should put our energy, for example in relation-building. It

23. Kansas University, "History of Strengths Perspective at KU."

also helped us to assess our community and determine that Waco did not have the strengths to adequately deal with languages other than English and Spanish. Therefore, we focused our ministry on Spanish-speakers only. In applying a strengths-based approach to support and care for asylum seekers, it is important to remember that immigrants have overcome great obstacles to get to where they arrived, living in a new land. A strengths-based approach builds on this reality and supports the asylum seeker in realizing their own inner strength and resourcefulness. It affirms their inherent dignity and worth and builds upon their talents, skills, and capabilities, seeking to guard against placing a different culture's goals or priorities onto them.

A strengths-based approach to support is also person-centered, meaning it seeks to make care and support personalized, coordinated, and empowering. It encourages the asylum seeker to take ownership of their care and support, involving them at every step of the way. One of the challenges with this type of approach is that it can be faster in the short term to make phone calls and appointments for them, for example, rather than going to the home and sitting with them while they make the phone call and navigate the system. Because our goal was building resiliency and empowerment, we learned it is important to take the time in the beginning to teach and walk alongside.

Another awareness revealed in the learning process was that it can be tempting to place our own North American middle-class expectations and goals upon those we support, which is a cultural expectation against which we must guard. Our new residents in the house do things differently than we do, and we must give space for that. Part of being person-centered in support and care also means placing the needs and dignity of the asylum seeker in high priority. This means holding confidences as much as possible, respecting their privacy, and letting them share their story when they wish. Because so many people in the congregation cared about them, their story, and their well-being, many naturally asked about how they were doing. This became a challenge to navigate, respecting privacy and confidences in a community living situation and in congregational ministry. We soon realized that it is always important to ask for permission first before sharing or moving forward with anything that relates to residents in the hospitality house.

Cultural Humility

Cultural humility requires critical self-awareness and is a process of ongoing self-reflection and self-critique of one's own biases and identities while also seeking to note power imbalances and one's role in them.[24] Cultural humility seeks to learn from others, recognizing that they are the experts of their own story and their own culture. When someone does something different from what we are accustomed to, we need to be curious and learn. We learned the wisdom of not assuming our way was the "right" way; instead, a humble approach seeks to learn from others. Humility is paramount in any endeavor of ministry, but especially for those who engage different cultures and ethnicities. Without humility, hospitality is not reciprocal and completely misses the biblical picture of hospitality as depicted in the Emmaus encounter with the risen Christ, a guest who became host, offering restoration and a new way of knowing Christ in the breaking of bread.

A long-standing ideology that exists in our country is that if immigrants come here, they should adopt the North American way of doing things.[25] This assumes that "our" way of being and thinking is best and should be adopted; while others' cultural beliefs and traditions should be left at the border. In helping volunteers identify these subtle patterns of thinking, we found it helpful to brainstorm about some of our cultural beliefs that we may not even recognize, such as our beliefs about education and parental involvement, language, time, family systems, and structures. We did not recognize all our strongly held cultural expectations until we started serving together and began to note the dissonance between "our" way of doing things and "their" way of doing them. We soon learned that anytime there was frustration or concern about how "they" were handling a situation, it became important to stop for a moment and be curious. We asked questions of ourselves, such as: Why am I concerned about this? What is going on in me in this situation? What are my strongly held beliefs here? Then, it became important to wonder about those same questions from the perspective of the immigrant and to consider what culturally held beliefs of ours might be impacting our visitors. Lastly, we began to ask which of our own cultural expectations and standards are not actually helpful or align with the gospel. Making space for processing these questions as a team during our work together, before reacting to situations, went a long

24. Sufrin, "3 Things to Know."

25. Evans, "Ethnocentrism in Psychology."

way in mitigating potentially damaging or hurtful reactions to the residents of the hospitality house.

In this chapter, I have described details of how we started and structured the ministry of a hospitality house for asylum seekers. I have briefly touched on the ways that we trained our laity for this ministry, much of which involved new learning and careful attention for those seeking to embark on this type of ministry. The basis of our ministerial approach rested upon our vision to companion the asylum seeker, understanding that each person bears the image of Christ. The calling to accompaniment developed over time, through exposure and study, and was an outpouring of our Christian vocational call to be the hands and feet of Christ in this place. Believing that in the sojourner we would meet Christ, we have looked forward to and sought the transformation of Christ among us. As Oscár Romero so eloquently described, in meeting Christ, we are transfigured. We realized that transformation is both a gift and result of sharing hospitality in this way. We came to believe the North American church needs to meet Christ, and we need this transformation of transfiguration. It can be a gift to the American church that the migrant church has come. Will we receive this gift of transformation?

5

Maintaining a Ministry and Thriving

Implementing a vision and leadership for a hospitality house calls forth many skills. Just because the sheetrock is up and the shingles are laid, the interior of the home painted and windows put in, does not mean the work is finished. All homeowners know that a lot of work is required to maintain a house. Homeowners must learn new skills to maintain the upkeep of their home, such as mowing and yard work, touching up paint and repairing holes in walls. Items in the home break and toilets clog. The same applies to maintaining a hospitality house, but the principle applies beyond the physical to emotional, mental, and spiritual maintenance. Building upon chapters 3 and 4 and the vision and calling that guided our church's creation of a ministry of hospitality, and the additional tools and wisdom we learned, this chapter addresses the skills that were called forth from us as we implemented this vision.

Andy Hogue and Gregory Jones argue that it is more important for leaders to be clear about their purpose than it is for them to create a mission or vision statement. Christian institutions often succumb to "mission drift" when they are not clear about their "why."[1] For this reason, we sought to keep our purpose paramount and to avoid getting too specific too soon about the details of what we wanted to do. Our purpose was to accompany the asylum seeker, extending the hospitality and peace of Christ. Flexibility and humility became critical virtues to adopt and skills to practice as the new ministry was birthed.

1. Hogue and Jones, *Navigating the Future*, 31–33.

Engaging in a hospitality ministry with those seeking asylum required our congregations to embody vulnerability in interactions with those who had been traumatized coming to the border. This meant showing deference, gentleness, and humility, while at the same time having healthy boundaries. At DaySpring, we sought to have our imaginations shaped by God's kingdom vision, always keeping our purpose and goal before us as we companioned asylum seekers in the love of Christ. We had to humbly seek new ways to interact with others and develop new skills.

Jones and Hogue urge leaders to stay close to their purpose and goal, instead of letting the particulars (who, how, and where questions) drive the conversation.[2] We tried to avoid the mission statement trap and stay flexible and learn as we went while holding to our main purpose to accompany asylees. Allowing purpose to direct leadership frees up the leader to practice innovation and improvisation.[3] Transformative leadership relies upon the purpose and goal to inform actions of practicality and structure. We as a congregation had to be mindful of this as we sought to create systems to sustain this ministry.

The work of ministry and hospitality called forth skills from me as a leader, from our leadership team, and from our congregation. We could prepare for some of these skills that were required of us, others we could not. Some we had to learn along the way. We learned conflict management as arguments erupted among the residents, we learned how to navigate systems of support in our community, how to seek help for victims of domestic violence and how to set boundaries when boundaries are pushed. We continue to learn how to create an effective "off ramp" as residents exit the house and start life on their own. It often feels like we are building the plane as we fly it. As we were building and flying at the same time, from my vantage point as a leader, I have been able to see congregants come alive with purpose in ministry.

One of the biggest disciplines we embraced during this leadership experience was to see challenges and obstacles as opportunities. We have been challenged to improvise, listen, and ask questions that get at the heart of the issue. We have had to guard against reacting, for every week there seem to be pressing and emergent needs to address.

2. Hogue and Jones, *Navigating the Future*, 33.

3. Hogue and Jones, *Navigating the Future*, 183–90.

Constraints as Opportunities

After months of praying, planning, and town hall meetings, the steering team was a bit discouraged that the original house offered for sale would not work. In *A Beautiful Constraint*, leadership authors Adam Morgan and Mark Barden suggest that constraints can often be beneficial and that we should learn how to make them beautiful, advantageous, or constructive. Being able to make this transition from scarcity to opportunity is a key definer of progress.[4] We challenged our team to see this constraint of going back to the drawing board in finding a house, as an opportunity. We took time to listen, to check in with some leaders in other ministries, and through this process, we were able to refine our vision and become much clearer about what we wanted to do. In deciding against buying a house, we clarified that we wanted to start out small, seek to build a replicable model, bring others along with us, and stay tethered to our church's core values (sacred and simple, renewal and rest) as much as possible. We decided we would start out renting a house or a duplex and give ourselves space and room to grow, and then expand later if our vision and desires grew. We wanted to guard against starting too big and then burning out.

This process of clarifying our vision served us well with our first challenges. Some of in the congregation felt that the church should start a nonprofit to coordinate this ministry. There were several compelling reasons for doing so: it might be simpler to allow a nonprofit to run it, and finances with the church would be separate. Additionally, some wondered if it might be easier to seek funding from other congregations and entities if the ministry were a separate nonprofit. These were important questions to listen to, discuss, and explore. Some downsides to starting a nonprofit might be that it could quickly become complicated (creating a board, applying for 501c3 status), and it could prevent the church from really taking ownership of the ministry. In the end, we relied on our vision to create a relational space where healing and restoration could happen (tied to one of the church's core values), and we would begin small and simple (tied to the other core church value). As a team, we decided to lean into the simple and relational aspect, knowing that we could always expand and create a non-profit down the road if we needed to do so. We desired to start a ministry that was a ministry of the congregation.

4. Morgan and Barden, *Beautiful Constraint.*

Other congregations with significant constraints were our inspiration for this. As mentioned, San Antonio Mennonite Church is a small church with limited resources, and they ignited our inspiration. For years in Waco, we have served alongside Cross Ties Ecumenical Church, a Church of the Savior Church that has about twenty members who run two significant ministries in town. One ministry, Talitha Koum, a therapeutic daycare, became a nonprofit, and the other is a ministry of the church: The Gospel Café, which partners with other churches in town to feed the homeless. This small and committed congregation has done amazing work with very limited financial and people resources. Their constraints have pushed them to become creative with how they engage with ministry and partner with others. These two congregations expanded our vision for what ministry might look like and how to embrace our constraints and look for opportunities within them.

One of the keys to transforming constraints into opportunities is keeping the ambition high[5] and the mission at the very forefront of your work. This challenged us to become clear about our goal and be able to communicate that well and often. We sought to help the congregation understand our purpose and goal of companioning the asylum seeker. Keeping our purpose in front of us and relying upon the models of these two modest churches helped us to transform the constraint of time and energy from the congregation.

In addition to time being a constraint, in some ways, our church motto, "sacred and simple," seemed prohibitive to some, of engaging in the messy and particularly human work of a hospitality house with asylum seekers. I heard often, "this is not simple." If one thinks of simple as being not-complicated, then yes, opening a hospitality house for asylum seekers is not simple. If one understands simple to mean removing all things that distract from what is sacred, distilling faith down to the essentials, then yes, opening a hospitality house for asylum seekers can be simple. It is a simple expression of what it means to follow Christ; it is at the heart of orthopraxy. Distinguishing and re-storying what "sacred and simple" means has been an important part of our conversations. I think some in the congregation had always understood simple to mean doing what is easy and small, whereas I think the heart of simplicity is doing what is essential and nothing else. We began to understand this ministry as being aligned with the core founding beliefs of the congregation. A hospitality house is an extension of who the

5. Hogue and Jones, *Navigating the Future*, 59.

church has always been. We have always been a place of healing and rest for weary souls, and a place of recovering faith that has been broken or exhausted. For us, the pilgrim church at our southern border epitomized those in need of restoration and rest. Extending care to the least of these, is an essential and "simple" demonstration of Christ's love in action.

Propelling questions have both a "bold ambition and significant constraint linked together"[6] and were a part of our clearly stated goals early on. A propelling question or goal for this hospitality and community home was, "How can we as a congregation create intentional Christian community and hospitality for the immigrant with our current full schedules and over busy lives?" Questions like this address the often unvoiced concerns and constraints head on, seeking to find a way through them together. It links constraints with goals and challenges leaders to be creative in moving forward. Morgan and Barden suggest that the "constraint is what we must use as a key parameter to meet this stretching ambition."[7] Given this statement, spending time with significant constraints by thinking about and exploring them, can be the key to linking them with ambitions and goals.

Our ambition was one of impact, which was rooted in a desire to minister to the alien or stranger, to those suffering and seeking a better life. It was a weighty prospect with a significant constraint (time and resources) that had constantly been a stumbling block to our "progress" in ministry in years past. This process of examining our constraints helped us to be clearer about our goals and ambitions in a way that inspired the congregation in ways not previously experienced before. When a congregation is on the precipice of a new experience in uncharted waters, it requires all the skills and creativity leaders can muster. Leaders must face constraints head on and seek to transform them into opportunities.

In *Navigating the Future*, Gregory Jones and Andy Hogue liken leadership to playing jazz. A good jazz musician has a strong foundation from which to improvise, adapt, and adjust.[8] Instead of creating mission statements that prescribe where an organization is headed, it suggests that, for leaders today, change happens so rapidly that organizations need to be nimble, adaptable, quick on their feet, and guided by their vision.[9] Flexibility and humility are paramount in leading an organization to create a

6. Hogue and Jones, *Navigating the Future*, 59.
7. Morgan and Barden, *Beautiful Constraint*, 65.
8. Hogue and Jones, *Navigating the Future*, 185.
9. Jones, *Christian Social Innovation*, 51.

new endeavor of a hospitality house. Flexibility allows leadership to adjust to constraints and find ways to transform them. Humility must be demonstrated at every step along the way, but it is especially critical as leadership addresses constraints and concerns and seeks to move around them while bringing people along and strengthening relational capital.

Leadership for Ministry

As this ministry unfolded, certain skills and leadership tools were called forth, both personally and from the congregation, we learned that leadership requires teachability. In addition to learning to view constraints as opportunities, we had to learn how to navigate and lead a ministry with so many different stakeholders. Letty Russell in *Just Hospitality* writes "[t]he ministry of service to humankind is the ministry of God in Christ reconciling the world."[10] This ministry is not ours; it is God's. Conversely, this ministry is not mine but the church's; this is the body of Christ in action. Even though I have been an instrumental part in the vision, creation, planning, foundation laying, building, framing, and maintenance, I often had to tell myself that his ministry was not my own, that it was the ministry of the church. At times, I needed to allow it to develop differently than what I had planned. That was my work to surrender and to humbly trust the process of the congregation. The minister's job is to equip saints for ministry in the world; this was so much of my job. I constantly had to discern when to let go and let others lead and when it was time to step in and guide.

A leader is someone who influences the ethos of some part of the world, be it a workplace, congregation, or even a family.[11] Leaders can create an atmosphere of trust and positivity, humility, and building upon strengths, which then creates an atmosphere of flourishing. Or, conversely, leaders can create systems of fear and distrust where unhealthy boundaries are evident. Our congregation is marked by grace and a high level of trust. It is the grace and trust that we have with each other that has kept this ministry alive. We have extended that to each other as we have led and served together. Without trust and grace from all aspects of the congregation, ministry like this would not flourish. Parker Palmer suggests that leaders must attend to their own shadows if they are to be effective leaders. This is where the work of spiritual formation for leaders is crucial. Leadership is a

10. Russell, *Just Hospitality*, 15 (paraphrasing Hans Hoekendijk).

11. Palmer, *Let Your Life Speak*, 3.

spiritual journey, which makes it perilous for leaders to neglect their own spiritual formation and mental well-being.

Transformative Leadership

Ongoing learning in our process revealed that, in Jesus Christ, three aspects of leadership are fully developed and realized—those of prophet, priest, and king. The *munus triplex*, or threefold office of Old Testament leadership, remains a guiding framework for Christian leaders today.

Prophets in the Old Testament cast a vision for what life in the kingdom of God should be, then called the people of God back to a God-centered life, which always included justice.[12] *Prophetic leadership* is imaginative, seeing through the fog, calling the people of God to a better way.

We realized the importance of considering how leaders might cast a vision for the congregation, of how they might embody Christ's companionship with the stranger and the outsider. This can be done through preaching, in pastoral prayers and liturgy, and through education. In pastoral prayers and preaching, ministers call followers to notice the unnoticed and to engage with those who suffer. This is part of prophetic leadership. Shame and guilt are de-motivating and must be guarded against; however, there are plenty of ways to be provocatively imaginative without the harshness sometimes seen in the prophets of old. Prophetic leadership sees what God is doing in the world, calls the people of God back to God, and challenges them to engage their faith.

Priestly leadership is also one of vision. The priest sees the divine in the ordinary acts of life; the priest brings God to the people.[13] Priestly ministry is vulnerable, relational, and sacrificial or kenotic. Christ emptied himself for us (Phil 2:7) as the ultimate act of priestly leadership. The incarnation and crucifixion exemplify priestly leadership. Christ came to walk among the suffering of the earth, exposed like us to the pain and indignities of humanity. Priestly leadership is vulnerable, faces suffering, and is changed by the suffering. Ultimately, Christ's vulnerability redeemed the suffering for all humankind through the cross and resurrection.

We understood that the church's engagement with the asylum seeker is relational and results in being stretched and changed. As leaders seeking

12. Hos 11:1–9; Mic 7:18–20; Amos 9:14–15; Jonah 4:2. See also Stevens, *Leadership Roles of the Old Testament*, 44–52.

13. Nelson, *Raising Up a Faithful Priest*, 105–88, 166–68.

to nurture the faith of the congregation toward being authentic followers of Christ, we were reminded to pay attention to the inner work that God needs to do in hearts and to the outer work toward which God calls us all. It is both inner and outer, as Parker Palmer suggests,[14] and it requires vulnerability. James McClendon also highlights leaders whose transformational leadership was birthed out of a "theology of character" as a reminder of this vulnerable task. God's work flowed out of their internal character development,[15] highlighting the importance of attending to our own inner work in preparation for ministry and service.

As Christians seeking to embody the love of Christ in ministry to the stranger and with the suffering, we experienced internal renewal, a necessary transformation for God's people. This required practicing vulnerability while learning to walk with those who suffer. It was messy as our lives were exposed to pain, frustration, and some level of chaos. Our church ethos of simplicity was challenged and yet it was an essential way in which the Holy Spirit blessed us and grew us. How can a leader prepare for the change that will inevitably occur in cross cultural ministry? As we communicated about the ministry, we continued to encourage openness to growing, learning from mistakes, and finding God in new and unexpected ways. These principles of spiritual growth have continued to guide us through this ministry-development process.

Kingly or royal leadership is also transformative, seeking to establish God's kingdom on earth. It is a kingdom where the last shall be first,[16] and Christ triumphs in death.[17] Royal leadership asks, "How can the church be God's instrument to bring about the kingdom of God?" It is an all-encompassing form of leadership that looks for the well-being of the people, seeking to establish structures that support well-being and human flourishing.

Throughout this process of developing a vision for a hospitality house, we strove to keep in mind the needs of those the church serves as well as the individual needs of congregants. Ministry of this type can be draining and discouraging at times and wonderful on other occasions. We learned to find ways to create structure and accountability so that the burdens did not

14. Palmer, "Leadership Begins Within."

15. McClendon, *Biography as Theology*, 2.

16. "For whoever wants to save his life will lose it, but whoever loses his life for My sake and for the gospel will save it" (Mark 8:35 NIV). "The last shall be first and the first shall be last" (Matt 20:16 NIV).

17. See also Kraybill, *Upside-Down Kingdom*, and Navone, *Triumph Through Failure*.

just fall on the shoulders of a couple of people. The emotional and spiritual health of everyone involved, not just the ones being served, is important to attend to. Imaginative, vulnerable, and transformative leadership are skills that we are continuing to learn on this leadership journey. Some of these skills were not intuitive, such as humility, vulnerability, and patience while seeking transformation. In working with our congregation, we experienced many different imaginations and ideas for how to go about the same calling and vision. This is where the work of humility, community, and listening all come together to forge a path forward.

Adaptive Leadership

In our preparatory research, we learned that adaptive leadership, according to Todd Bolsinger in *Canoeing the Mountains*, is about energizing a community toward its own transformation to accomplish a shared mission. This transformation must involve listening to the marginal voices. Bolsinger provides the example of how explorers Lewis and Clark's survival depended upon listening to Sacagawea in their uncharted explorations. Listening to marginal voices empowers the community by helping them recognize their value and their own influence.[18] It is about elevating leadership and calling out gifts in one another. Faithful adaptive leadership empowers others to see their liabilities as their assets and looks for the marginal voices in the congregation. It involves listening to those who are minorities, to those in the immigrant community, and learning from them and their lived experiences. This will only strengthen the church's ministry.

Part of adaptive leadership is being able to say "yes, and" while also seeking to ask the best questions. It is a mindset of receptivity, flexibility, and curiosity. "Yes, and" is a guideline in improvisational comedy. Hogue and Jones in *Navigating the Future* highlight the importance of improvisation in leadership in this new millennium. In improv comedy, the comedian is trained to take what is given to them and then improvise and add to it, essentially saying "yes, and." The comedian does not know where the skit will ultimately land but improvises on the spot.[19] Similarly, in ministry leadership, something new and creative presents itself daily. Listening to and understanding concerns and ideas is an important part of addressing roadblocks and constraints on the spot and then finding a way forward. We

18. Bolsinger, *Canoeing the Mountains*, 193.

19. Hogue and Jones, *Navigating the Future*, 185–90.

are constantly trying to say "yes . . . and" as we encounter new challenges and ideas while still keeping our eyes focused on our vision of sharing in hospitality with the immigrant.

With the divergent culture becoming our norm,[20] a renewed vision for Christian leadership is needed, one that is relational, empowering, and courageous. In this new era of learning to navigate the post-Christendom waters "off the map," the church and its leaders must ask, "What is God doing and how might God be inviting us?" This work of discerning God's guidance and direction requires that we as leaders and as the church, attend first to our own relationship with God. This is personal but also more importantly in the context of leadership in the church, it is communal. Effective and adaptive Christian leadership can use the tools and gifts of spiritual direction, which help find opportunity in challenge, facilitate honest community and relationships, and enhance our spiritual growth. These are unprecedented times for the church; however, we have the tools we need and the learned experiences of those who have been overlooked that can help guide the church to adapt and live into its calling to be the people of God for the sake of the world.

This journal entry below describes a time in which I needed to adapt my leadership, to listen to the marginal voices around me, and I was better for it. I invited a Latina woman who I knew to visit with me. I wanted her perspective, and I extended an invitation to help us lead this ministry.

> Journal: Welcome Dinner
> "How are you going to welcome the families? What will they eat for their first meal?" One of Hispanic leaders involved in our ministry asked me this question. We are opening a hospitality house; some call them welcome houses. Our whole goal is to welcome. She also told me that sometimes it is hard for her to come to our church when no one else at the church looks like her. We met for coffee because I wanted to hear her perspective. I wanted her thoughts on how we might extend hospitality. We have a welcome bag for each guest and some clothes in their drawers, a stuffed animal for each child and a handmade blanket. She said, "You need their first meal to be comfort food, food from their country. I'll make it. Just let me know where they are from, and I'll make the food and bring it." Brilliant idea. I am so glad that I reached out to her to hear her ideas and perspective. She has been an invaluable partner in this ministry. We have learned a lot from her and in turn our ministry is better.

20. Willimon, *Leading with the Sermon*, 25.

Group Dynamics

Another aspect of ongoing learning involves studying the life cycle of a group, for many factors influence how a group functions. One constraint with leading in a congregation is that everyone is a "volunteer," in addition to their own vocations and family responsibilities. The opportunity found within this constraint is that because it is voluntary, there is sometimes a higher degree of passion for the work. The life cycle of a group model explains that as a group or team develops maturity and stability, and relationships are formed, the leadership style can morph or change to a more collaborative or shared leadership. The cycle moves from forming, storming, norming, and performing to adjourning.[21] In our work with the ministry of the Naomi House, the leadership team had to take a stronger leadership role for our ministry team in the beginning. At that time, we modeled collaboration, a strengths-based approach, and set boundaries by not attempting to meet every need that arose with our asylee neighbors in the house.

In the forming stage, group members are new, trying to understand their roles and that of the team. They are adjusting to personalities and what is most likely quite a new ministry experience. In this stage, teams are trying to assess needs and establish boundaries of what their team can do and how much they can personally give. In the storming stage, groups work to get organized, developing tasks and processes to meet needs. Conflicts arise as passions are high and clarity is still developing. During the norming phase, some experiences give way to establishing better ways of doing and being together. Leadership becomes more shared, and a higher level of trust is established. This is a period of high creativity and collaboration. The performing stage is marked by true interdependence and flexibility. It is adaptable and highly productive. In the adjourning stage, there is a significant change in the structure and people move on or take breaks. This is a time to think purposefully about how to successfully onboard new team members and reform.[22]

Conflict is inevitable in any group work, and for our team, it was no different. In our new ministry, there was often a high level of investment and emotional connection. Learning about conflict management was a necessity as well as developing healthy patterns of communication for the ministry

21. For more on Tuckman's *Life Cycle of the Group*, see Westchester University, "Tuckman's Stages of Group Development."

22. Westchester University, "Tuckman's Stages of Group Development."

team. This necessarily starts at the top, with leaders modeling humility and listening. When tensions were high, it is important to remind ourselves that, for many of us, this type of ministry was a holy calling. It was helpful to practice having generous assumptions and modeling trust within the group. Even in the best of circumstances when leaders have done all the preventative work, there are times when negativity can seep in and become detrimental to group work. Creating healthy feedback loops allows team members to share concerns, ideas, or feedback in non-threatening ways. We provided opportunities for team members to share ideas and then "park ideas" in "parking lots," so to say, and come back to them. Tuckman encourages avoiding back-chat—talking about others or leaders or problems behind others' backs. This only leads to confusion and misunderstandings, and it destroys trust. Susan Beaumont exhorts to not allow negativity to fester, and instead encourage team members to go straight to the source for clarification.[23]

Communication was essential as the team developed, and as the church embarked on our new endeavor. We saw the need to keep retelling the story, even though it had been said before, as new people, who do not know the history of the church, the history of the process, or the vision, continually join the congregation. Continued communication, and at times what might feel like overcommunication, was essential.

Spiritual Formation for Flourishing

Beaumont, in *How to Lead When You Don't Know Where You Are Going*, urges leaders to tend to the soul of the institution as they lead by: 1) listening, 2) attending to discernment together by paying attention to what God is doing within the congregation, 3) paying attention to the collective stories that are told about past and present, and 4) considering how that impacts the emerging stories for a hope-filled future.[24] She urges church leaders to pay attention to their soul work individually and corporately, seeking ways to attend to the guidance of the Holy Spirit. She uses the framework of spiritual direction to guide her style of leadership. Spiritual direction often asks such questions as, "Who are we?" "What is God calling us (or me) to do, to be, to believe, to become?" "Who are we here to serve?"

In paying attention to soul care of individuals and congregations, we also learned that it is imperative to remember rest and sabbath. Ministry

23. Westchester University, "Tuckman's Stages of Group Development."

24. Beaumont, *Leading When You Don't Know Where You Are Going*, ix–x.

with the asylum seekers, with those on the margins of society who are reduced to bare life, is too important for burnout. Ministers and lay leaders must attend to their own needs and souls to maintain longevity in this important work.

In *Emotional Intelligence for Religious Leaders*, authors John West, Roy Oswald, and Nadyne Guzman address equipping ministers for longevity in ministry.[25] Emotional self-awareness is crucial to being able to lead by influence because this type of leadership flows out of the core of who leaders are; it relies upon their own sincerity. There is no way to "fake it"; therefore, we must spend the time and energy to be spiritually grounded and emotionally healthy.

In the beginning, a series of town hall meetings gave the congregation and the steering team opportunities to diffuse tension and anxiety about such a new endeavor. It was important to listen to people's concerns, take them seriously, and invite them in the process, even when those planning had already thought of and addressed the concerns. At these town hall conversations, each table recorded their hopes and concerns about the project. In subsequent meetings, church members divided into groups to think through and address specific components of the ministry such as church engagement, hospitality, community living, finances, training and equipping, immigration concerns, and information. These subgroups spent time thinking, asking important questions, and doing research, after which they reported back to the larger team.

Longevity and Replication

Keeping our end goals in mind, to accompany the asylum seeker and to create a replicable model, have helped the ministry team stay focused. Articulating clear goals empowered our ministry teams to say no when necessary. Burnout is commonplace in ministry, especially in ministries of this sort, but the work is too important to burnout in two years. Setting clear boundaries about what the ministry could and could not do was crucial. It was also important for individuals to have a clear sense of their own boundaries. Many well-meaning people have been sucked into the black hole of serving in ways that are more "doing for" than "doing with." Steve Corbett and Brian Fikkert warn against this type of paternalism, writing:

25. West et al., *Emotional Intelligence for Religious Leaders*.

"Do not do things for people that they can do for themselves."[26] We learned that unintentional "doing for" others can lead to frustrated and overworked volunteers and frustrated and unempowered residents in the hospitality house. Susanna Snyder cautions those serving with immigrants that there are ways to give that can fill their hands but break their spirits. Some benign ways of giving can be destructive. Mutuality needs to be at the center of all encounters between your church and immigrants, and in such a way that leads to relationship and friendship.[27] Avoiding paternalism is crucial for both longevity in ministry and creating a replicable model.

Over the years, as this ministry has evolved, the guiding principles of playing to our strengths and seeing constraints as opportunities have been welcome guides that have allowed us to stay in ministry for the long-haul. When national policies changed, we took the opportunity to adjust our model, seek simplicity and try something new. By focusing on what we know we can do well, we could build ministry around that. Some of our strengths grew to become a Spanish language Sunday school class, a bilingual night of worship in the hospitality house and English practice hour on Sunday afternoons. We have sought longevity in this ministry and in doing so we have been able to let go of aspects of the ministry that may not have been a strength for us. Very few ministries of this sort remain the same. They seem to always be in a state of improvement, adjustment and tweaking. With continued changes to the national implementation of immigration policies and the asylum process, our church will have to continue to re-evaluate our ministry and discern our calling and adapt. While re-evaluating and adjusting the ministry we always remind ourselves that we cannot fix the immigration problem, and we cannot save nor help everyone. We can only be faithful to God's calling, doing our small part in bringing about God's kingdom here on earth.

John Wesley's three simple rules are instructive for all Christians and are often used as a part of baptismal services. They are also especially prudent for those in ministry of this sort: "Do no harm. Do good. Stay in love with Jesus."[28] In "doing no harm," we ask if this action or policy will do harm, whether intentional or not. Sometimes actions can be harmful when we disregard other's feelings or needs, when we do "for" and not "with," or when we are compelled by compassion without some forethought. For

26. Corbett and Fikkert, *When Helping Hurts*, 109.

27. Snyder, *Asylum-Seeking*, 198.

28. Job, *Three Simple Rules*.

example, if there is a dog on the side of the interstate, a compassionate heart might immediately stop to grab the dog without thinking first about how to do it in the safest way possible so as not to endanger other drivers. Sometimes, our quest to do good can lead to harm if we are not thoughtful about what and how we are doing.

As a part of the baptismal covenant in many traditions, the admonition, "Do good" is followed by, "We will, with God's help." Seeking God's best for others is at the heart of both ministry and the Christian life. Sometimes our ideas of what is best may not exactly align with what God sees as good and right. The only ways to mitigate this are to stay tethered to Christian community and to experience God through Scripture, worship, and prayer. The goodness that the Christian life produces is the good fruit of a life filled with the Holy Spirit.

"Stay in love with Jesus" is essential for all who serve Christ in ministry of this sort. It is imperative to attend to one's own spiritual growth, health, and development. It is so easy to get caught up in doing good, that one becomes worn out, exhausted, jaded, and bitter. Christians must make their spiritual and emotional health a priority; it is the very sustenance that we all need. Flight attendants have it right—in case of an emergency, put on our oxygen masks first before helping others do the same.

We came to see that ministry with those in poverty and crisis can quickly become complicated. We learned, as much as possible, to keep things simple, paired down, and basic, and to set boundaries whenever possible. Saying no and avoiding trying to be all things to all people helps prevent burnout, which is hard to do in crisis-related ministries, but it is necessary for longevity and replication.

Worship and Liturgy

The word liturgy means "the work of the people." Through our liturgy, we work out our theology and our faith, speaking and singing what we know until we believe it in our hearts. Our liturgy shapes us and molds us in Christlikeness. Isaac Villegas wrote about performing liturgies for those who died crossing the US–Mexico border in Arizona, noting that their liturgy is the labor of a group in service to the community, saying: "Our liturgy is for the community of the dead, to join our lives to theirs in a remembering."[29] Liturgy teaches, remembers, forms, and shapes us. It

29. I. Villegas, "Liturgy in the Borderlands."

teaches us to draw all things into the presence of Christ who is with us. In liturgy, we worship God in the ordinary moments, making sacred and holy all that is normal and routine.

Worship is the primary means through which the church teaches and spiritually forms the congregation. As leaders and ministers, we must consider how worship leads the people of God to embrace the calling of God to be God's ambassadors of peace and mercy. The hymns that are sung, Scriptures read, and prayers offered all play a part in forming the Christian soul and heart. The simplest place to begin is by including responsive readings or litanies from the Psalms and prophets. Responsive readings engage the congregation as they repeat the words of God, layering the learning from hearing and speaking. We should not shy away from Psalms of lament, either. Some of the harder or more raw passages are an important part of helping the laity to identify their own suffering and loss. This is a crucial step to beginning to embrace those who are suffering. This is how empathy is born. Submitting to the entirety of Scripture, specifically the Psalter and the prophets, forms congregants in seeing God's heart for the suffering, for mercy and justice.

In summary, a key virtue that was called forth from us in this work was humility. For Augustine, humility is the central Christian virtue and the "antidote to pride" and is crucial to being able to understand justice.[30] Humility can grow as the Holy Spirit transforms listeners through the hearing of Scripture in worship situated within a practicing Christian community. Worship is the primary means through which Christians are formed and shaped for ministry in the world and can be an integral part in developing hearts for ministry.

30. Bretherton, *Christianity and Contemporary Politics*, 143–44.

6

Bearing Witness: A Theological and Pastoral Reflection

In conclusion, I want to offer a theological and ministerial perspective that will give this type of ministry a robust depth as churches seek to embody Christ's love and presence. Following Christ's life and teachings to be the dynamic people of God more fully, we must extend ourselves on behalf of the "least of these," the poor and needy, the stranger, and those overlooked. In doing this, the church can encounter God, for the poor are fitting vessels for God's presence and power.[1] It is necessary for our faith growth, and it is necessary for all those who suffer, that the church would it extend itself in this way as a part of denying itself, taking up the cross, and following Christ. Cardinal Joseph W. Tobin sums up the immigration predicament for the church today: "Refugees and migrants risk losing their lives. The rest of us could lose our souls."[2] In serving those seeking refuge, the church may well find itself anew, as it rediscovers and lives into its purpose and telos.

Bearing Witness

How should a congregation reflect theologically on the work of hospitality ministry with asylum seekers? Two words that give voice to many different

1. Colón-Emeric, *Óscar Romero's Theological Vision*, 250–69.
2. Francis, *Stranger and You Welcomed Me*, xiii.

approaches to incarnational ministry are *presence* and *witness*. We seek to be present to others as God is present to us and we are bearing witness to the continual work of the Holy Spirit among us. Through a ministry of presence, we also bear witness to the pain and suffering of our neighbors who come seeking refuge. This bearing witness is a holy task. The migrant church is knocking at our door, asking for help. When we believe that we meet Christ in the stranger, and when we believe that we are transformed by looking into the face of Christ as in the transfiguration, then we understand that this work is about bearing witness to God's work among us. We do not create the bounty, but the Holy Spirit does. We create space for trauma healing, we open our hearts, our homes, and our congregation in hospitality, and God moves.

Witnessing automatically implies a relationship. It gives voice to the suffering so that the one suffering knows they are not alone. Seeing and being with in the suffering is an act of compassion and care.[3] Hospitable witnessing makes space for the story to unfold; it is a way of bearing witness to pain and joy. It is a ministry of presence that embodies the presence of Christ. Reverend Sam Wells came to this same realization through his work with those experiencing homelessness in London. He suggests that the heart of so many of our breakdowns in relationships and in society hinges on "being with" others instead doing "for."[4]

"Wicked problems" such as homelessness or mass migration, for example, are social or cultural problems that are almost too difficult to solve because of their complexity. Wicked problems lack clarity in their aims or pursuits.[5] Wells asserts that *being with* is expressly rooted in the gospel, for Emmanuel means "God *with* us." In John 1:14, the word, Christ, became flesh and lived *with* humanity. The temptation to fix and to do *for* others is pervasive and enticing. Ministers, parents, and advocates become so busy trying to fix complex problems and doing for others that they neglect to simply *be with* them. Neglecting relationship building is so easy because it is the more uncomfortable and challenging work. It requires time and vulnerability, it is not often obvious, simple or up front, and it does not garner much praise and attention.

3. Oh, *Hospitable Witnessing*, 1.

4. Wells, "Being With" (St. Martin-in-the-Fields). See also Wells, "'Being With'" (Diocese of Oxford).

5. *Interaction Design Foundation*, "What Are Wicked Problems?"

With Christ as a guide, *being with* is an important lens through which to view and fashion a ministry with asylum seekers. A ministry of presence or being with sets the foundation for being able to bear witness to and lament with the immigrant. It creates space for God's work of redeeming pain and brokenness to flourish.

Witnessing is a communal act that makes room for the voice of the suffering. Hospitable witnessing attends with compassion and care and seeks to stand in solidarity with those who are suffering.[6] French philosopher Simone Weil made "attention" (*l'attention*) a fundamental component of her work. Paying deep attention, for Weil, is arduous but leads to discernment. This type of paying attention "includes discerning what someone is going through in her or his suffering" with a posture of readiness to receive what it is that God or the object of the attention has to offer.[7] This type of attention-keeping is part of what it means to bear witness with the asylum seeker. It means spending time with, listening to, walking alongside of, and gazing into their lives, ready to receive and learn from them. In doing so, we will encounter God in new ways, for we trust that God will meet us in this moment, enabling us to bear witness to God's work in and around the immigrant.

We encounter the hospitable God of Scripture as we open ourselves to the work of the Holy Spirit in and around us, in the asylum seeker.[8] Smither traces a thread of missional hospitality throughout Scripture and through Christian history.[9] It is this radical and ordinary hospitality that creates an environment of faithful presence, listening, and mutuality in which God is known and made known. It may well be the antidote to our postmodern, cynical culture that sees no need for the church.

As Christian leaders, we are called to bear witness to the reign of God. This is complex, and to do so, we must imagine beyond what we can see. The church cannot engage the world as the hands and feet of Christ without a robust spiritual imagination. At times it does seem like many in the church have lost their spiritual imagination. North American culture's crisis of imagination has been fueled by dualistic thinking[10] and rapidly changing

6. Oh, *Hospitable Witnessing*, 8.

7. *Stanford Encyclopedia of Philosophy*, "Simone Weil."

8. Smither, *Mission as Hospitality*, 6.

9. For a good literature review of current work on biblical hospitality from all angles, see Smither's first chapter of *Mission as Hospitality*.

10. See Richard Rohr for more on how dualistic thinking manifests itself today: Rohr, "Dualistic Mind."

cultural mores so that Christians are left confused seeing no viable answers or solutions to the complex problems of today. Dualistic thinking is binary thinking or often what some call "black and white thinking": us versus them, good versus bad. In our politics and in our churches, it often demonizes the other and can impede bridge-building and creativity. As leaders, we ought not to get bogged down in what often feels like the traps of dualistic thinking and cultural battles; rather, we would do well to seek creative solutions to difficult predicaments. We must guard against letting culture influence our discipleship and orthopraxy. Caring for immigrants and the vulnerable is clearly a scriptural mandate that the church must continue to enact even if the dominant culture says otherwise. Dualistic thinking is prevalent in the political discourse about immigration. There is an inability to see, for example, how our laws could be compassionate and yet also secure the border. Solutions to complex problems such as immigration require courage, creativity, and collaboration. The church is blessed with rich theological resources in Scripture and tradition that have the power to challenge and transform dominant cultural discourses in ways that offer solutions to "wicked" problems.

Fostering creativity has been a critical part of developing the ministry of the Naomi House. Focusing on strengths, listening, learning, we leaned-in to the challenges and sought creative ways to address challenges. Some of these creative solutions and approaches have been the result of generative conversations with asylum seekers themselves. As we bear witness and pay attention to the immigrant, we may just find that new and creative options exist that may not have been obvious at first glance. We may receive energy, and the church may be enlivened by this prolonged, open-hearted gaze.

When one thinks about bearing witness, one might traditionally think of evangelism and attesting to the reign of God, winning souls over for Christ. In my context, witnessing is also about receiving and being with, in which space we learn to see what God is doing around us. We get to witness God's healing work around us. We pray, "Lord may your kingdom come, may your will be done, on earth as it is in heaven," and when we do so we are acknowledging that God's work is happening now. It is often hard to see, and so our challenge is to learn to see it. A failure of imagination is causing the North American church to miss the migrant church that has come to the border, potentially offering a fresh expression of faith and dependency upon the suffering Christ that we need. It is a pure gift to watch the work of God in restoring brokenness and bringing a family back to life. There is no credit in this for the hospitality house or church members, or the church. It is purely the work of the Holy Spirit that we witness. In opening oneself up to relationships, in opening a hospitality house, the church gets a front-row seat to God's work of healing and restoration. It is God at work in ways that are not always obvious in our insulated and distracted lives. Bearing witness requires a reorientation of life, a slowing down and making space for relationships, for the sharing of stories, and for God's work to unfold. It is not expedient or efficient, and it can be messy. These may be some of the biggest barriers to encountering God in this way. It does not always fit into our neatly devised categories and time slots.

In *Life Together*, Bonhoeffer makes the case that Christians must live out their faith in a community that has at its center participating in the transformation of God's world. Christian community always meets the felt needs of the hurting world, in which we greet the sick, the prisoners, and those in "exile" as if they are Christ. This is a weighty reality and yet, conversely, both the companioned and the one companioning find that they "recognize in each other the Christ who is present in the body . . . they receive and meet each other as one receives the presence of the Lord."[11] Humility, meekness, and forbearance are forged in the hard work of building relationships. It is not a rosy picture of life together, but rather one marked with challenge and joy, patterned after the life of Christ.[12] Bonhoeffer goes on to describe how Jesus Christ is our brother, and we are to receive others as his and our brothers, forgiving and restoring just as Christ has done for us. Expounding on Rom 15:17, we are to meet others as he has met us.[13] This is a sobering reminder of the challenges of life together and the gift of meeting Christ in the midst of this discipline of building community.

Oscar Romero's response to the endemic and dominating violence in El Salvador was liberation or freedom found in the transfiguration of Christ. For him, salvation means transfiguration: all who encounter Christ are changed and liberated to bring the "light of Christ to all men," imparting dignity and hope and reinvigorating vocation.[14] This same transfiguration is for all today who will gaze long enough at Christ—whose face is also found in the immigrant today. This is the gift of bearing witness to God's activity in the life of the foreigner or stranger.

11. Bonhoeffer, *Life Together*, 20.

12. Bonhoeffer, *Life Together*, ch. 5 "Ministry."

13. Bonhoeffer, *Life Together*, 25.

14. Colón-Emeric, *Óscar Romero's Theological Vision*, 76.

Cardinal Joseph Tobin, in the introduction to Pope Francis' collection of homilies, *A Stranger and You Welcomed Me*, wonders about the rising level of despair reflected in the US's high suicide and violence rates and the connection with a growing hardness of heart toward the plight of immigrants. He writes, "Failure to recognize and respond to hope hardens our hearts and disfigures our faces."[15] Is it possible that Americans' failure to engage in care and empathy hardens us and leads to despair?

St. Bernard of Clairvaux and St. Catherine of Sienna both address the need for God's work of renewal and conviction in our own hearts, for if we cannot see or be in touch with our own suffering and need for mercy, then we cannot extend mercy. Pope Francis made a similar point: "The more conscious we are of our wretchedness and our sins, the more we experience the love and infinite mercy of God among us, and the more capable we are of looking upon the many 'wounded' we meet along the way with acceptance and mercy."[16] Receiving God's mercy in all its fullness enables us to give that same mercy away. Having experienced suffering, we are more prone to have compassion for the suffering. The engagement, or lack thereof, of the Christian church with those who suffer, with asylum seekers specifically, is directly related to our spiritual formation. When the church does not engage in extending mercy and justice, it is a sign of inward spiritual atrophy and soul malformation.

Weil's deep gaze or attention upon those who suffer can lead or move God's people to action in solidarity with those who have suffered trauma. This deep attention is fertile ground for hospitality and hospitable witness. Priscilla Oh suggests three Christian practices that embody hospitable witnessing: care for others as made in the image of God, compassion as being present with those suffering, and lament as a way to give voice to the suffering and move all towards hope.[17]

Lament is the spiritual practice in which we seek to discover how God is present amid painful realities of trauma, calamity, and violence. Nina Balmaceda observes that "Lament is the school of authentic hope"[18] and is a crucial part of opening the heart's door to healing. Lament creates space for spiritual communication with God and can help prevent feelings of isolation, especially when it is used in a corporate setting. It can be a discipline

15. Francis, *Stranger and You Welcomed Me*, xiv.

16. Sri, "Mercy Melts 'Hidden Sin.'"

17. Oh, *Hospitable Witnessing*, 13–16.

18. Balmaceda, "Word Made Flesh."

to create space in our liturgy and in our prayers to express sorrow over all that has gone wrong. Why is this important? Lament reminds us to face reality and to bring the healing presence of Christ into our areas of pain.[19] In accompanying those seeking asylum, you surely will have cause to lament. You will feel their pain, you will see and experience the ramifications of an unjust society, and you will lament the complexity of this kind of ministry. I have found that lamenting with God can lead to deeper spiritual transformation and growth.

Carlos Colón, a modern liturgist, and hymn writer, originally from El Salvador, writes music and prayers that express the laments of refugees and asylum seekers. He gives voice to the voiceless and you can explore some of his work on his website.[20]

Hymns and songs of lament are not often sung in worship, nor are they even easy to find. Lament is scriptural and is a discipline that can be enlivening, opening the door for the healing and reconciling work of the Holy Spirit.

We do not have to gaze too long to be overwhelmed by all there is to lament. In lament, we bear witness to what is happening and give voice to it. We sit with it and let the Holy Spirit work in us through it. This is hard: we are often compelled to jump in and fix it, or to gloss over the pain and focus on the positive, or to avoid and neglect the sorrow. It is uncomfortable, but what if in the discomfort and in the voicing of our pain and lament, of our anger and hurt, we might discover something new? In opening our hearts in lament to God, we may find a new freedom from the pain and a path to God's inbreaking healing and restoration in our own lives, and in the world. Scripture provides many healthy examples of lament from the Psalms to Job to Naomi, who changed her name to Maura, meaning bitter, to Jesus on the cross crying out, "My God, why have you forsaken me?" (Matt 27:46 NRSV; Ps 122). Our Christian tradition teaches us to lament, to cry out to God, and doing so often opens doors for courage to grow and for healing to begin.

Accompanying the asylum seeker in mutuality and humility creates space for relationships to flourish. In doing so, we catch glimpses of the Holy Spirit at work reconciling and healing. Bearing witness to the work of God among those seeking refuge is a balm that soothes those weary with lament. God's inbreaking kingdom, God's new creation is nowhere more

19. For more on recovering lament as a practice, see Swenson, *Living Through Pain*.

20. https://carloscoloncomposer.com/.

evident than in ministry with those seeking refuge and asylum. Maybe this is because God chose to align with immigrants, by coming as a child and living the life of one seeking refuge. Our destination on this journey of life is God's kingdom, where all are welcomed to the banquet table, where every nation and tongue will praise God together. On this earth, the church is Christ's body helping bring about this beautiful vision and calling, which is already and not yet. God is drawing all people in, but it is not yet fully realized. This is where we are going.

Where is the hope? In our work with the Naomi House, we have had a front-row seat to God's work of healing and restoration in broken lives and hurting families. We have seen hearts once opposed to God transformed by God's grace and enduring presence in the pain. We have seen an invigorated and enlivened faith in our congregants. We have experienced those who were once worn out and turned off by religion finding new meaning and reconciliation with God. We have seen traumatized families find their footing through the loving arms of the Christian community. We have experienced asylum seekers who once received from the ministry, now leading and organizing the ministry. We have seen churches of all denominations and ideologies rally together in ministry. We have discovered a new hope through all the ways that the Spirit of God is reconciling hearts, families and congregations. Nina Balmaceda, with the Center for Reconciliation at Duke University, shares that the virtue of hope is sometimes likened to a mother who has two daughters: anger and courage. Anger at the way things are, and courage to see that things can change.[21] Anger that has been transformed through lament can lead to courage to change terrible realities. Bearing witness with our fellow pilgrims seeking safety and refuge is the beginning to uncovering new ways of encountering God, which is precisely what the church needs in the continual unfolding of God's inbreaking kingdom in our present reality.

Congregations who embark on the journey of companioning asylum seekers stand on a solid biblical foundation of welcoming the stranger and offering hospitality to the foreigner. Throughout the history of the church, Christians have cared for the poor and the overlooked, and in fact, it has been one of the defining aspects of Christianity that has shaped culture and set the church apart from other institutions. Christians have exhibited courageous leadership in caring for the persecuted, the refugee, the

21. At times this quote has been attributed to St. Augustine, but it has recently been disputed. See also Balmaceda, "Word Made Flesh."

overlooked, and the neglected. Churches seeking to build a ministry of accompaniment with asylum seekers have much to offer their congregation in the way of teaching and training for this ministry. Even in our culture of polarization, ministry of this sort is possible, and it is enlivening for the church caught in the sea change of post-Christendom.

Leadership in this era of the church requires new skills of adaptation to rise to the challenge of moving forward in creatively sharing the hope and love of Christ. In an era of unprecedented political turmoil and mass migration that will only continue to increase due to climate and governmental corruption, the church must find a way to engage this crisis in a way that leads to life, restoration, and hope for the millions who are seeking refuge and safety all over the world. In doing so, a gift awaits the church, which is the chance to bear witness to and participate in God's work of healing, reconciling, and restoring lives. It is a gift that will enliven and invigorate the church if we will let it. The only requirement is that we show up and open our hearts in hospitality, echoing the words of Mary, "I am the servant of the Lord. May it be unto me according to your word."[22] God is at work, and the migrant church is here, knocking on our doors.

22. Luke 1:38.

Appendix I

Questions for Reflection

Chapter 1: Introduction

- What has drawn you and your group to reading this book?

Chapter 2: Laying the Foundation

The resource of guiding questions listed below for chapters 2–5 can be employed by congregations in developing their own programming around these issues. They can also be used for group discussion and personal reflection after reading the material of each chapter. They can be very useful for a team or congregational leaders exploring a calling to extending hospitality to asylum seekers.

Part 1: Pastoral and Theological Preparation: Equipping the Leader/Minister

- How have you experienced hospitality? Describe different kinds of hospitality that have been shared with you or that you shared with another.

- How does the understanding of the *imago Dei* impact how you see others?
- Find a hospitality or welcome house near you and visit it. Listen and learn from them.
- What practices help foster hospitality?
- What are some practices you can adopt to train yourself and your community to practice hospitality?
- How does your theological lens propel you to share the love of Christ and to minister to the suffering . . . or not?

Part 2: Biblical and Historical Preparation: Equipping the Congregation

- How do we recover what it means to be a pilgrim people?
- How do you view God differently as you look at the Old Testament through the lens of migration? How might you see God as one who accompanies refugees?
- How might Mary's prayer, "Let it be," impact how you understand holy hospitality?
- How might we prepare for our own suffering and then empower each other to go to the suffering? In what ways do you see this happening?
- How have you received hospitality from others? From Christ? Is there an image or story that embodies Christ's hospitality for you?
- Help your congregation observe "Las Posadas," enacting the Holy Family's search for hospitality and reflect on what it is like to deny and be denied hospitality.
- How would our lives look different if we really took to heart the idea that all Christians are "resident aliens"?
- What is the invitation from God after this study? What do we seek in ministering with asylum seekers?
- Read and discuss *The Bible and Borders* by Daniel Carroll or *Seeking Refuge* by Stephen Bauman et al.

- Consider now how you might guard against setting your own expectations upon asylum-seekers that you will begin sharing your life with. How might you begin preparing now to embody cultural humility?

Chapter 3: Developing Blueprints and Setting the Structure

- How are you ready for change and growth?
- How can you get clear on what is your work to do?
- Where is the anxiety? What is motivating this endeavor?
- How can you clarify, simplify, and stay flexible?
- How might God want to birth something in you? What does it mean to be hospitable to God's work in you? Mary gave consent for God to use her. What does a fully yielded Christ follower look like? How would you describe this kind of life?
- What can we do well? Evaluate your strengths and limitations both personally and corporately.
- How can we extend hospitality and not slip into fixing someone else's problems?
- How do you identify and honor high levels of investment in your congregation and laity?
- Write a litany based on Scripture, drawing attention to God's mercy with those who suffer.
- What are the needs in your community for immigrants?
- What are your strengths and growing edges personally? As a team? As a congregation? As a community or town?
- What passages in Scripture are your guiding passages as you consider embarking on a journey of hospitality with asylum seekers or refugees?
- Go somewhere (restaurant, grocery store, event), where you are the minority and you do not speak the language. Notice how you feel and what you experience. Attend another church where you do not speak the language.
- Prayer: Lord, help me receive what comes at me today with grace and wisdom.

Chapter 4: Maintaining the House: The Skills that Were Called Forth

- What is your purpose in beginning a ministry of this sort? How can you keep your purpose paramount and not get bogged down in details?
- What constraints do you have as you begin this ministry? How might you be able to turn those into an opportunity?
- What skills are you developing personally as a leader? What new skills are being called forth from you as a congregation?
- In what ways have church leadership demonstrated prophetic, priestly, or kingly leadership?
- How can you listen to the marginal voices around you? What are they saying about ministry with immigrants?
- How can your ministry avoid paternalism and seek mutuality and relationship?
- How have you experienced the life cycle of a group before?

Chapter 5: Conclusion: Theological and Pastoral Reflection

- How have you seen the Holy Spirit at work around you as you prepare for and engage in ministry with immigrants?
- What have you learned about God from people of a different culture?
- How can you make space for lament? What are your laments? Write a prayer of lament.
- What gives you hope? Describe the hope that you experience in building relationships with immigrants.

Appendix II

Resources: Choruses, Prayers, Litanies

The hymnal *Santo Santo Santo Holy Holy Holy: Cantos para el pueblo de Dios Songs for the People of God* is a great worship resource with songs, choruses and hymns that are easily sung in both Spanish and English. Some of the litanies and prayers below have been used in worship at DaySpring Baptist Church in Waco, Texas. With gratitude we hope that they are useful for others in worship.

World Relief has a helpful prayer guide for congregational use. https://worldrelief.org/wp-content/uploads/2025/02/World-Relief-Prayer-Guide.pdf.

Litanies and Prayers

Renewing our Covenant Together

Brothers and Sisters, God has not called us to journey alone but to walk hand in hand.

Let us reach out to one another in faith and friendship.

We have been welcome into God's family.

Let us extend welcome and open arms to one another with hope and hospitality.

We are being transformed by the love of God made known in Christ.

Let us embody that love to one another and to our neighbors.

We are a part of God's Church, the Body of Christ.

We offer our time, our unique gifts, and our resources to God's work in this place.

We commit ourselves to Christ's ministry of redemption.

We covenant, as a people of faith, to worship and walk with one another.

We have renewed our commitments.

Let us be faithful even as God is faithful. Amen.

Come and Worship

In the midst of a world where people hunger and thirst,

come worship a God who feeds the hungry.

In the midst of a world where people are abused and oppressed,

come worship a God who calls for compassion and justice.

In the midst of a world filled with war and rumors of war,

come worship a God who desires only peace for the world.

In the midst of a world of spiritual emptiness,

come worship a God who gives life meaning.

Come, worship our God whose grace and love know no end.

Call to Worship from Psalm 146

I will praise the Lord all my life

I will sing praise to God as long as I live

God upholds the cause of the oppressed

And gives food to the hungry

The Lord lifts up those who are bowed down

The Lord watches over the foreigner

The Lord reigns forever

Let us worship the Lord. Hallelujah, Amen.

Prayers

O Lord, forgive my sins against my sisters and brothers.

Where I have created walls around my heart . . . have mercy.

Where I have been hesitant to know . . . have mercy.

Where I have labeled and condemned . . . have mercy.
Where I have been too afraid to be honest . . . have mercy.
And grant me your grace that I may love . . .
Those who are different than I am,
Those who are in need of my time,
Those who have hurt me or offended me,
Those who may not love me back.
In the presence and power of Jesus, I pray.
(unknown)

Prayer of Confession

Lord, we confess our need for your grace. We do not always do the things we know are right to do. We have sinned and humbly ask for your forgiveness.
Forgive us if we have been callous. **Give us compassion.**
Forgive us if we have been lazy. **Give us inspiration.**
Forgive us if we have been too afraid. **Give us courage.**
Forgive us if we have been selfish. **Give us generosity.**
Forgive us if we have been dishonest. **Give us integrity.**
Thanks be to God, **Through Jesus Christ our Lord we are forgiven.**
(unknown)

Merciful God, we confess that we have been unfaithful to you
and unloving to those around us.
When those in need have cried out for help,
we have turned our backs upon them,
and in so doing
have shut the doors of our hearts
to your love for them through us.
Forgive us and may the mercy we receive
be apparent in the lives we live.
Through Christ, our Lord,
Amen.
(unknown)

Prayer for weapons to be turned to instruments of abundance and peace (Isaiah 2:4)

An Advent Prayer

Holy God, We come with thankful hearts for your presence in our lives and for your abundant provision. We thank you for baptisms and hearts turned towards you, for families and the servant hearts of the faithful of God who are living testimonies of your goodness. Most of all, we are thankful that through Jesus Christ you forgive our sin and call us to you. We are grateful God, that you redeem and restore all things and we continue to seek that restoration in our own lives and in this world. As we enter this Advent season, we pray that you would cause us to turn our distracted hearts towards you and grow in us a fervent love for you as we wait. We hold our gratitude mixed with concern for all that is not right in this world. O Lord there is a famine of peace and a pervasive hunger for meaning and justice. We lament and pray for you to make all things right. With the prophet Isaiah, we long for weapons to be turned into instruments of peace and abundance and we long for all to realize your just and righteous love. We give to you today our grateful and our heavy hearts. Take and heal us, that we may be your people in this place who choose to reflect your light and love in all ways. Amen.

Pastoral Prayer—Darkness to Light

O Lord where there is darkness bring light, where there is violence bring peace, where this is brokenness mend hearts and minds and bring healing and restoration. Where there is despair bring hope where there is hunger and thirst provide sustenance, where there is anger bring a softening and acceptance of you. Nothing is too far gone that you cannot redeem and restore.

O Lord our hearts lament at the corruption, violence, and pain of this world, that cause so many to flee their homes. Our hearts lament for lives that are hurting and broken. Lord may your kingdom come on earth, as it is in heaven. Bring justice and empower your Church to be your agents of mercy. Help us O Lord to see how we might be your hands and feet.

We give you thanks for calling upon us and for how you have empowered us through the Holy Spirit to serve in ways we never would have thought possible. We are humbled by your faithfulness Lord and rely upon you for all things. To you O God, be all honor and glory through Jesus Christ. Amen.

Prayer of Being Light-Bearers

Holy and Almighty God, to you, we lift our hearts today.

You created us in your image and through Jesus Christ we have been set free to walk in new life. We lay down our sorrows and confess our need for you today, clinging to your promise that you will make all things new. For all who are in need of your healing and renewal, we pray. Will you give us eyes to see the hurting and all who are in need of your light and love that we may be your instruments of love in this place.

We offer ourselves to you today in worship. We praise you for your love that will never let us go. Fill our hearts with your praise, may the Holy Spirit be evident teaching, uniting, and consoling — drawing us all to you. For the sake of your kingdom come on earth, shape us in Christ-likeness that we may love you more dearly and be your light-bearers to a world in need, through Jesus Christ our Lord, Amen.

Prayer of Lament and Thanksgiving

Lord of Life and Love,

We echo the prayers of the Church this week as we live in a world where all is not right and yet it is also a world of beauty, where we catch glimpses of Your grace, mercy, and creativity.

For all that is broken . . . we lament

For all that is a gift . . . we give thanks

Our hearts are heavy for the brokenness on display this week. For the people of Afghanistan and Haiti who suffer unbearable calamity, war, and violence. Where there is despair bring hope, relief, and healing. Strengthen the people of God to minister in these places of deep hurt. For the many homeless in our city, for immigrants waiting in shelters and refugees fleeing violence O Lord have mercy. Lead us Lord in how to respond in Christ-like love to the challenges of our world.

For the gift of being co-laborers with Christ—sharing in your wide mercy and love, for the assurance that we are never alone, even on the darkest of nights and when we cannot see nor sense your presence God, you are with us. We give thanks. For the gift of life and love in Christ—a gift we do not deserve and have not earned. You, O Lord, heal brokenness and redeem pain. Take our reluctant and distracted hearts and breathe new life and love into our lives. You can take a humble and repentant heart and make a saint. For all this, we give thanks.

For all that was broken, we lament

For all that is a gift, we give thanks

For our past that haunts us and for grief that still lingers

For the sins of our ancestors that still plague us today—we lament and seek your healing.

For the gifts of family, friends and mentors who have guided us into your light. For the relationships you have mended and lives you have redeemed and healed . . .

For the testimony of your faithfulness in the lives of the saints and all the unsung heroes of the faith who have held high the Christ light for us—we give thanks.

For all that will be broken, we lament

For all that will be a gift, we give thanks

The trials that this world brings will continue:

Violence and injustice, sin and brokenness, the lure of consuming and pacifying to make ourselves feel better, the enticements of this age and the age to come we lament and ask that you strengthen us to stand fast and ever cling to you. Give us grace and mercy to live with the mystery of a fallen world, held in the hands of You, our good and loving Creator.

For the people of God who will continue to seek ways to live faithfully as your people.

For the ways you will reveal yourself to a new generation and for your love for all people that will not tire we give thanks. Guide us Lord as we seek to be gift, as we seek to be your hands and feet bringing hope and light for those seeking asylum. Be in our planning and praying, guiding, and teaching us how to receive and give the hospitality of Christ.

We ask all these things in the name of Our Lord and Redeemer, Jesus who is the Christ and who reigns with you O Lord God and the Holy Spirit, one God now and forever. Amen.

Quotes

The social thought and the social practice inspired by the Gospel will always be characterized by a sensitivity towards those who suffer most, those who are extremely poor, those who are overwhelmed by all the physical, mental and moral evils that afflict humanity, including hunger, contempt, unemployment and despair. You need to look for the structural causes that promote the different classes of poverty in the world.—Pope John Paul II[1]

RESOURCES

https://traumahealinginstitute.org/
https://socialwork.web.baylor.edu/c3i
https://immigrationforum.org/
https://isaacvillegas.com/words/
https://carloscoloncomposer.com/choral-music-2/
https://www.faithward.org/migration-and-immigration-church-resources/
https://worldrelief.org/resources/
https://faithworks.com/

1. Romero, *Through the Year with Oscar Romero*, viii

Bibliography

Abdelkader, Engy. “Immigration in the Era of Trump: Jarring Social, Political, and Legal Realities.” *The Harbinger* (Volume 44). https://socialchangenyu.com/harbinger/immigration-in-the-era-of-trump-jarring-social-political-and-legal-realities/.

Agamben, Giorgio. *Homo Sacer: Sovereign Power and Bare Life*. Stanford, CA: Stanford University Press, 1995.

Ainsley, Julia. “Migrant Border Crossings in Fiscal Year 2022 Topped 2.76 Million, Breaking Previous Record.” *NBC News*, October 22, 2022. https://www.nbcnews.com/politics/immigration/migrant-border-crossings-fiscal-year-2022-topped-276-million-breaking-rcna53517.

American Immigration Council. “Asylum in the United States.” August 2022. https://www.americanimmigrationcouncil.org/sites/default/files/research/asylum_in_the_united_states_0.pdf.

Atwood, Craig D. “Catechism of the Bohemian Brethren.” *Journal of Moravian History* 2 (2007) 91–117.

Bae, Junghun. *John Chrysostom: on Almsgiving and the Therapy of the Soul*. Paderborn: Ferdinand Schöningh Verlag, 2021.

Balmaceda, Nina. “The Word Made Flesh: Seeking Transformation and Reconciliation.” *International Fellowship for Mission as Transformation*, March 11, 2021. https://infemit.org/word-made-flesh/.

Barna Group. “Atheism Doubles Among Generation Z.” Barna.com, January 24, 2018. www.barna.com/research/atheism-doubles-among-generation-z.

Barton, Ruth Haley. *Discerning God’s Will Together* by Ruth Haley Barton. Downers Grove, IL: InterVarsity, 2012.

Batalova, Jeanne. “Top Statistics on Global Migration and Migrants.” *Migration Policy Institute*, July 21, 2022. https://www.migrationpolicy.org/article/top-statistics-global-migration-migrants.

Bauman, Stephen, et al. *Seeking Refuge: On the Shores of the Global Refugee Crisis*. Chicago: Moody, 2016.

Baylor University. “Trauma.” https://socialwork.web.baylor.edu/research-impact/center-church-community-impact-c3i/how-we-do-it/resources/trauma.

———. “Trauma-Sensitive Congregations.” https://socialwork.web.baylor.edu/research-impact/center-church-community-impact-c3i/trauma-sensitive-congregations.

Beaumont, Susan. *Leading When You Don’t Know Where You Are Going*. Lanham, MD: Rowman & Littlefield, 2019.

Benner, David. *Opening to God*. Downers Grove, IL: InterVarsity, 2010.

Bill, Brent. *Sacred Compass*. Brewster, MA: Paraclete, 2009.

Blume, Laura. "Honduras: A Narco-State Made in the United States." NACLA, April 17, 2024 https://nacla.org/honduras-narco-state-made-in-the-united-states/.

Bodenner, Chris. "Losing Your Faith After Seeing So Much Suffering." *The Atlantic*, March 30, 2016. https://www.theatlantic.com/notes/2016/03/losing-your-faith-after-seeing-so-much-suffering/476064/

Boesak, Allan. "To Stand Where God Stands: Reflections on the Confession of Belhar after 25 Years." In *Belhar Confession: The Embracing Confession of Faith for Church and Society*, edited by Mary-Anne Plaatjies-Van Huffel and Leepo Modise, 421–39. Stellenbosch: African Sun Media, 2017. http://www.jstor.org/stable/j.ctv1nzgoxm.28.

Bonhoeffer, Dietrich. "The Church and the Jewish Question." In *Dietrich Bonhoeffer Works*, edited by Larry Rasmussen and translated by Isabel Best and David-Higgins, 12:365. Minneapolis: Fortress, 2009.

———. *Life Together*. New York: Harper Collins, 1954.

Bolsinger, Todd. *Canoeing the Mountains: Leadership in Uncharted Territory*. Downers Grove, IL: InterVarsity, 2018.

Bretherton, Luke. *Christ and the Common Life: Political Theology and the Case for Democracy*. Grand Rapids: Eerdmans, 2019.

———. *Christianity and Contemporary Politics: The Conditions and Possibilities of Faithful Witness*. Hoboken, NJ: Wiley & Sons, 2010.

———. *Hospitality as Holiness: Christian Witness Amid Moral Diversity*. New York: Ashgate, 2016.

Burge, Ryan P. "Only Half of Kids Raised Southern Baptist Stay Southern Baptist." *Christianity Today*, May 24, 2019. https://www.christianitytoday.com/news/2019/may/southern-baptist-sbc-decline-conversion-retention-gss.html.

Busch, Eberhard. *The Barmen Theses Then and Now: The 2004 Warfield Lectures at Princeton Theological Seminary*. Grand Rapids: Eerdmans, 2010.

Canning, Raymond, trans. *Augustine of Hippo: Instructing Beginners in Faith*. The Augustine Series 5. Hyde Park, NY: New City, 2006.

Carr, Simonetta. "Gregory of Nyssa: A Lone Voice Against Slavery." *Place for Truth*, August 11, 2020. https://www.placefortruth.org/blog/gregory-of-nyssa-a-lone-voice-against-slavery.

Carroll R., M. Daniel. *The Bible and Borders: Hearing God's Word on Immigration*. Grand Rapids: Brazos, 2020.

Catechism of the Catholic Church. "7 Spiritual and 7 Corporal Works of Mercy." https://fwdioc.org/works-of-mercy.pdf.

Catherine of Siena, *The Dialogue*. Translated by Suzanne Noffke. New York: Paulist, 1980.

The Catholic Worker Movement. "About the Catholic Worker Movement." https://catholicworker.org/about-the-catholic-worker-movement/.

Chalmers. "When Helping Hurts: The Small Group Experience." https://chalmers.org/resources/books/when-helping-hurts-the-small-group-experience/.

Claassens, Juliana, et al. *Restorative Readings: The Old Testament, Ethics, and Human Dignity*. Eugene, OR: Pickwick, 2015.

Clemot, Ellen Clark. *Discerning Welcome: A Reformed Faith Approach to Refugees*. Eugene, OR: Cascade, 2022.

Colón-Emeric, Edgardo. *Óscar Romero's Theological Vision: Liberation and Transformation of the Poor*. Notre Dame: University of Notre Dame Press, 2018.

Conde-Frazier, Elizabeth, et al. *Latina Evangélicas: A Theological Survey from the Margins.* Eugene, OR: Cascade, 2013.

Corbett, Steve, and Brian Fikkert. *When Helping Hurts: How to Alleviate Poverty without Hurting the Poor and Yourself.* Chicago: Moody, 2009.

Dillard, Annie. *Teaching a Stone to Talk: Expeditions and Encounters.* New York: HarperCollins, 1982.

Dodd, Patton. "A Texas Congregation Caring for Immigrants Gains a New Understanding of Christianity as a 'Trauma-healing Movement.'" *Faith and Leadership,* January 21, 2020. https://faithandleadership.com/texas-congregation-caring-immigrants-gains-new-understanding-christianity-trauma-healing-movement.

Doran, Robert. *Stewards of the Poor: The Man of God, Rabbula, and Hiba in Fifth-Century Edessa.* Kalamazoo, MI: Cistercian, 2006.

Doughty, Stephen V., and Majorie J. Thompson. *Companions in Christ: The Way of Discernment.* Nashville: Upper Room, 2008.

Dutch Reformed Mission Church in South Africa. "Confession of Belhar." 1986. https://www.presbyterianmission.org/wp-content/uploads/Confession-of-Belhar-text-2016.pdf.

Edlow, Joe. "Biden's 'Abolish ICE' Agenda Puts American Lives at Risk." *Fox News,* Nov. 27, 2023. https://www.foxnews.com/opinion/bidens-abolish-ice-agenda-puts-american-lives-risk.

Ellsberg, Robert, ed. *Dorothy Day: Selected Writings.* Maryknoll, NY: Orbis, 1983.

Erickson, Erik. "Social Justice: Both Sides Are Doing It Wrong." *Clarion Ledger,* October 12, 2018. https://www.clarionledger.com/story/opinion/columnists/2018/10/12/social-justice-both-sides-doing-wrong/1613285002/.

Evans, Olivia Guy. "Ethnocentrism in Psychology: Examples, Disadvantages, and Cultural Relativism." *Simply Psychology,* September 22, 2023. https://www.simplypsychology.org/ethnocentrism.html.

Floyd, Shawn. "Aquinas and the Obligations of Mercy." *The Journal of Religious Ethics* 37 (2009) 449–71.

Francis, Pope. *A Stranger and You Welcomed Me: A Call to Mercy and Solidarity with Migrants and Refugees.* Maryknoll, NY: Orbis, 2018.

Fryling, Alice. *Seeking God Together.* Downers Grove, IL: InterVarsity, 2008.

Gaultiere, Bill. "Four Degrees of Love." *Soul Shepherding.* https://www.soulshepherding.org/bernard-of-clairvauxs-four-degrees-of-love/.

Garland, David E. *Mark.* NIV Application Commentary. Grand Rapids: Zondervan, 1996.

———. *A Theology of Mark's Gospel: Good News About Jesus the Messiah, the Son of God.* Grand Rapids: Zondervan, 2015.

Garland, John. "Fleeing North in the Full Armor of God." *Christianity Today,* June 18, 2019. https://www.christianitytoday.com/ct/2019/june-web-only/migrant-san-antonio-border-trauma-therapy.html.

González, Karen. *Beyond Welcome: Centering Immigrants in Our Christian Response to Immigration.* Grand Rapids: Brazos Press, 2022.

Gramlich, John. "Monthly Encounters with Immigrants at the U.S.-Mexico Border Remain Near Record Highs." *Pew Research,* January 13, 2023. https://www.pewresearch.org/fact-tank/2023/01/13/monthly-encounters-with-migrants-at-u-s-mexico-border-remain-near-record-highs/.

Guterres, António. "Women on the Run: Full Report." United Nations High Commission on Refugees. https://www.unhcr.org/56fc31864.html

Haillie, Phillip P. *Lest Innocent Blood Be Shed: The Story of the Village of Le Chambon and How Goodness Happened There*. New York: Harper & Row, 1979.

Harmless, William. "Review of Augustine of Hippo: Instructing Beginners in Faith." *The Catholic Historical Review* 93 (2007) 611–12.

Harris, Tiffani. "Building Stronger Communities and Economies Starts with Immigration Reform." *Waco Tribune Herald*, November 9, 2023. https://wacotrib.com/opinion/column/tiffani-harris-building-stronger-communities-and-economies-starts-with-immigration-reform/article_a7f590be-7da0-11ee-bc3d-2700664648c6.html.

———. "In Central Texas, the Naomi House Makes Me Proud to Be a Baptist Again." *Baptist News Global*, October 7, 2022. https://baptistnews.com/article/in-central-texas-the-naomi-house-makes-me-proud-to-be-a-baptist-again/.

Hauerwas, Stanley, and William Willimon. *Resident Aliens: Life in the Christian Colony.* Nashville: Abingdon, 2014.

Hogue, Andrew P., and Gregory L. Jones. *Navigating the Future: Traditioned Innovation for Wilder Seas*. Nashville: Abingdon, 2021.

Holman, Susan. *The Hungry Are Dying: Beggars and Bishops in Roman Cappadocia*. New York: Oxford University Press, 2001.

Holocaust Encyclopedia. "United States Immigration and Refugee Law, 1921–1980." https://encyclopedia.ushmm.org/content/en/article/united-states-immigration-and-refugee-law-1921-1980.

Huffel, Mary-Anne Plaatjies Van. "The Belhar Confession: Born in the Struggle against Apartheid in Southern Africa." Paper from University of Stellenbosch. Stellenbosch, South Africa. http://www.scielo.org.za/pdf/she/v39n1/07.pdf.

The Humming Bird or Morsels of Information, on the Subject of Slavery with various Miscellaneous Articles. Leicester, England: A Cockshaw (1825). https://www.google.co.uk/books/edition/The_Humming_bird_or_Morsels_of_informati/FL4PAAAAQAAJ?hl=en&gbpv=1.

The Humming Bird. "Address to the Ladies of Great-Britain in Behalf of the Negro-Slaves." 1 (1825) 201.

———. "The Illegality of the Slave Trade." 1 (December 1824). https://www.google.co.uk/books/edition/The_Humming_bird_or_Morsels_of_informati/FL4PAAAAQAAJ?hl=en&gbpv=1.

Interaction Design Foundation. "What Are Wicked Problems?" https://www.interaction-design.org/literature/topics/wicked-problems#.

Ivereigh, Austen. *Wounded Shepherd: Pope Francis and His Struggle to Convert the Catholic Church*. New York: Henry Holt, 2019.

James, Felicity, and Rebecca Shuttleworth. "Susanna Watts and Elizabeth Heyrick: Collaborative Campaigning in the Midlands 1820–34." In *Women's Literary Networks and Romanticism*. https://academic.oup.com/liverpool-scholarship-online/book/43414/chapter/363238222.

Ji, Li-June, et al. "Cultural Differences in the Construal of Suffering and the COVID-19 Pandemic." *Social Psychological and Personality Science* 12 (2021) 1039–47.

Jipp, Joshua W., and Christine Pohl. *Saved by Faith and Hospitality*. Grand Rapids: Eerdmans, 2017.

Job, Rueben. *Three Simple Rules*. Nashville: Abingdon, 2007.

Johnson-Miller, Beverly C., and Benjamin D. Espinoza. "Catechesis, Mystagogy, and Pedagogy: Continuing the Conversation." *Christian Education Journal* 15 (2018) 156–70.

Jones, Greg. *Christian Social Innovation.* Nashville: Abingdon, 2016.

Jones, Robert P. *The End of White Christian America.* New York: Simon & Schuster, 2017.

Joseph, Celucien L. "One More Word About the Gospel, Culture, Marxism, and Social Justice." *The Witness*, April 15, 2019. https://thewitnessbcc.com/one-more-word-about-the-gospel-cultural-marxism-and-social-justice/.

Kalantzis, George. *Caesar and the Lamb.* Eugene, OR: Cascade, 2012.

Kansas University. "History of Strengths Perspective at KU." https://socwel.ku.edu/history-strengths-perspective#.

Kilby, Karen, and Rachel Davies, eds. *Suffering and the Christian Life.* London: T. & T. Clark, 2020.

Ko, Susan. "Promoting Culturally Competent Trauma-Informed Practices." *National Center for Child Traumatic Stress Culture and Trauma Brief* 1 no. 1 (2005) n.d.

Kraybill, Donald B. *The Upside-Down Kingdom.* Harrisonburg, VA: Herald, 2018.

Lefebure, Leo D. "The Understanding of Suffering in the Early Christian Church." *Claritas: Journal of dialogue and Culture* 4 (2015) 29–37.

Lenhart, John M. "Catechetical Instruction in the Eastern Church." *Franciscan Studies* 14 (1954) 81–105.

Levine, Amy-Jill, and Marianne Blickenstaff, eds. *A Feminist Companion to Mark.* Sheffield, UK: Sheffield Academic Press, 2011.

Lipka, Michael. "A Closer Look at America's Rapidly Growing Religious 'Nones.'" *Pew Research Center*, May 13, 2015. https://www.pewresearch.org/fact-tank/2015/05/13/a-closer-look-at-americas-rapidly-growing-religious-nones/.

Longenecker, Bruce. *Remember the Poor: Paul, Poverty and the Greco-Roman World.* Grand Rapids: Eerdmans, 2010.

Longenecker, Bruce, and Kelly Liebengood, eds. *Engaging Economics: New Testament Scenarios and the Early Christian Reception.* Grand Rapids: Eerdmans, 2009.

Lupton, William, and Joseph Downing. *The Necessity of Positive Duty . . . A Sermon Preach'd in the Parish-Church of St. Sepulchre, June the 5th, 1718. Being Thursday in Whitsun-week, at the Anniversary Meeting of the Children Educated in the Charity-schools in and About the Cities of Long and Westminster.* London, 1718.

MacIntyre, Alasdair. *After Virtue: A Study in Moral Theory.* Notre Dame, IN: University of Notre Dame Press, 1984.

———. *Dependent Rational Animals: Why Human Beings Need the Virtues.* London: Duckworth, 1999.

MacMaster, Llewellyn L. M. "Standing Where God Stands (Outside the Gate, with Christ): The Belhar Confession as a Call for Public Pastoral Care." In *Belhar Confession: The Embracing Confession of Faith for Church and Society*, edited by Mary-Anne Plaatjies-Van Huffel and Leepo Modise, 273–94. Stellenbosch: African Sun Media, 2017.

Mason, George. "John Garland Prefers the Term 'Pilgrim' Instead of 'Immigrant.'" *Good God Podcast*, October 21, 2021. https://goodgodproject.com/podcast/season7episode1.

McClendon, James. *Biography as Theology: How Life Stories Can Remake Today's Theology.* Eugene, OR: Wipf & Stock, 2002.

Meilaender, Peter. *Toward a Theory of Immigration.* New York: Palgrave MacMillan, 2015.

Montañez, Daniel, and Wilmer Estrada Carrasquillo, eds. *The Church and Migration: A Theological Vision for the People of God.* Cleveland, TN: Centro para Estudios Latinos Press, 2022.

Morgan, Adam, and Mark Barden. *A Beautiful Constraint: How to Transform Your Limitations into Advantages, and Why It's Everyone's Business.* Hoboken, NJ: John Wiley & Sons, 2015.

Mukpo, Ashoka. "Nicaragua Failing to Protect Indigenous Groups from Land Grabs." Mongabay, May 4, 2020. https://news.mongabay.com/2020/05/nicaragua-failing-to-protect-indigenous-groups-from-land-grabs-report/

Murphy, David. "Moving Beyond Trauma: Child Migrants and Refugees in the United States." *Child Trends,* September 2016. https://www.childtrends.org/wp-content/uploads/2016/09/Moving-Beyond-Trauma-Report-FINAL.pdf.

Navone, John. *Triumph Through Failure: A Theology of the Cross.* Eugene, OR: Wipf & Stock, 2014.

Nelson, Richard D. *Raising Up a Faithful Priest: Community and Priesthood in Biblical Theology.* Louisville, KY: Westminster John Knox, 1993.

Nessan, Craig L. "Barmen Confession: Learning from the Barmen Declaration of 1934: Theological-Ethical-Political Commentary." *Journal of Lutheran Ethics,* December 1, 2019. https://elca.org/JLE/Articles/1292.

Newman, Elizabeth. *Untamed Hospitality: Welcoming God and Other Strangers.* Grand Rapids: Brazos, 2007.

Nouwen, Henri J. M. *Turn My Mourning into Dancing: Finding Hope in Hard Times.* Nashville: Thomas Nelson, 2001.

———. *With Burning Hearts: A Meditation on the Eucharistic Life.* Maryknoll, NY: Orbis, 1998.

O'Connell, Gerard. "Sister Norma Pimental: Be an Instrument of Faith for Migrants and Refugees." *America: The Jesuit Review,* September 28, 2017. https://www.americamagazine.org/faith/2017/09/28/sister-norma-pimentel-be-instrument-faith-migrants-and-refugees.

Oden, Amy G. *And You Welcomed Me: A Sourcebook on Hospitality in Early Christianity.* Nashville: Abingdon, 2001.

Oden, Thomas C. *Mark.* Ancient Christian Commentary on Scripture, NT 2. Downers Grove, IL: InterVarsity, 2005.

Oh, Priscilla Sung Kyung. *Hospitable Witnessing: Using Autoethnography to Reflect Theologically on a Journey of Friendship and Mental Health Problems.* Eugene, OR: Pickwick, 2018.

Palmer, Parker J. *Let Your Life Speak: Listening for the Voice of Vocation.* San Francisco: Jossey-Bass, 2000.

———. "Leadership Begins Within." *Center for Courage and Renewal.* https://couragerenewal.org/library/leading-from-within/.

PBS News. "Climate Change Is Already Fueling Global Migration. The World Isn't Ready to Meet People's Changing Needs, Experts Say." July 28, 2022. https://www.pbs.org/newshour/world/climate-change-is-already-fueling-global-migration-the-world-isnt-ready-to-meet-peoples-needs-experts-say.

PCUSA. "The Confession of Belhar with References." October 1, 2013. https://pcusa.org/resource/confession-belhar-with-references.

Perez, Edwin J. "The Study of Liberation Theology in Latin America." Eddie Perez, August 2, 2018. https://breachingthewalls.org/2018/08/26/the-study-of-liberation-theology-in-latin%E2%80%8B-america/.

Perkins, Robert L., ed. *Practice in Christianity.* Macon, GA: Mercer University Press, 2004.

Plaatjies-Van Huffel, Mary-Anne, and Leepo Modise, eds. *Belhar Confession: The Embracing Confession of Faith for Church and Society*. Stellenbosch: African Sun Media, 2017.

Pohl, Christine D. *Making Room: Recovering Hospitality as a Christian Tradition*. Grand Rapids: Eerdmans, 1999.

Posner, Michael. "Why the Biden Administration Needs to Preserve the Right to Asylum." *Forbes*, February 27, 2023. https://www.forbes.com/sites/michaelposner/2023/02/27/why-the-biden-administration-needs-to-preserve-the-right-to-asylum/?sh=3ddb366f698b.

Rasmussen, Larry L., ed. *Dietrich Bonhoeffer Works: Berlin 1932–1933*. Translated by Isabel Best and David-Higgins. Minneapolis: Fortress, 2009.

Reed, Angela H., et al. *Spiritual Companioning: A Guide to Protestant Theology and Practice*. Grand Rapids: Baker Academic, 2015.

Rendel, *Leading Change in the Congregations: Spiritual and Organizational Tools for Leaders*. Lanham, MD: Rowman & Littlefield, 2019.

Rescue.org. "Is It Legal to Cross the U.S. Border to Seek Asylum?" July 1, 2022. https://www.rescue.org/article/it-legal-cross-us-border-seek-asylum#.

Rhee, Helen. *Loving the Poor, Saving the Rich: Wealth, Poverty, and Early Christian Formation*. Grand Rapids: Baker Academic, 2012.

Richardson, K. C. *Early Christian Care for the Poor: An Alternative Subsistence Strategy Under Roman Imperial Rule*. Eugene, OR: Cascade, 2018.

Roach, David. "Why Southern Baptists' Social Justice Spat Is Actually About the Sufficiency of Scripture." *Christianity Today*, August 7, 2019. https://www.christianitytoday.com/news/2019/august/founders-doc-southern-baptists-social-justice-scripture.html.

Rochester, Stuart. *Self-Denial: A New Testament View*. Eugene, OR: Cascade, 2019.

Rohr, Richard. "The Dualistic Mind." The Center for Action and Contemplation, January 29, 2017. https://cac.org/daily-meditations/the-dualistic-mind-2017-01-29/.

Romero, Oscar. *The Scandal of Redemption: When God Liberates the Poor, Saves Sinners, and Heals Nations*. Edited by Carolyn Kurtz. New York: Plough, 2018.

———. *Through the Year with Oscar Romero*. Translated by Irene B. Hodgson. Cincinnati: Franciscan Media. 2005.

———. *The Violence of Love*. Compiled and Translated by James R. Brockman. Walden, NY: Bruderhoff, 2003.

Romero, Robert Chao. *Brown Church: Five Centuries of Latina/o Social Justice, Theology, and Identity*. Downers Grove, IL: InterVarsity Press Academic, 2020.

Rowe, C. Kavin. *Christianity's Surprise: A Sure and Certain Hope*. Nashville: Abingdon Press, 2020.

———. "Kavin Rowe: Recovering the Surprise of Christianity." *Faith and Leadership*, October 2020. https://faithandleadership.com/kavin-rowe-recovering-surprise-christianity.

———. "Suffering Is Part of Thriving." *Faith and Leadership*, April 7, 2014. https://faithandleadership.com/c-kavin-rowe-suffering-part-thriving

Rowlands, Anna. "On the Promise and the Limits of Politics: Faith-based Responses to Asylum Seeking." In *Fortress Britain? Ethical Approaches to Immigration Policy for a Post-Brexit Britain*, edited by Ben Ryan, 70. Philadelphia: Jessica Kingsley Publishers, 2018.

———. "The Politics of the Common Good: Contemporary European Challenges and Opportunities." *Modern Believing* 61 (2020) 37–51.

———. "Temporality, Dispossession and the Search for the Good: Interpreting the Book of Jeremiah with Jesuit Refugee Service." *Political Theology* 19 (2018) 517–36.

———. "What Is Mercy? Part 3: Building Community." Durham University, September 8, 2020. https://www.youtube.com/watch?v=EHyHhkdM_f4.

Russell, Letty M., et al., eds. *Just Hospitality: God's Welcome in a World of Difference.* Louisville, KY: Westminster John Knox, 2009.

Ryan, Ben, ed. *Fortress Britain? Ethical Approaches to Immigration Policy for a Post-Brexit Britain*. Philadelphia: Jessica Kingsley, 2018.

Salvatierra, Alexia. "Dolorisimo or Orthopathos? Latin American Theologies of Suffering." *Fuller Studio.* https://fullerstudio.fuller.edu/dolorisimo-or-orthopathos-latin-american-theologies-of-suffering/.

Sandlin, P. Andrew. "A Primer on Cultural Marxism." *Journal of Christian Legal Thought* 8 (2018) 10. https://www.christianlegalsociety.org/wp-content/uploads/2022/08/CLSJournal_Winter2018_web.pdf.

Santo Santo Santo Holy Holy Holy: Cantos para el pueblo de Dios Songs for the People of God. Chicago: Gia Publications, 2019.

Shoemaker, Stephen. "Does the Church Need a New Barmen Declaration?" *Baptist News Global,* July 27, 2021. https://baptistnews.com/article/does-the-church-in-america-need-a-new-barmen-declaration/#.Yp53sZPMLAM.

Silliman, Daniel. "Decline of Christianity Shows No Signs of Stopping." *Christianity Today,* September 13, 2022. https://www.christianitytoday.com/news/2022/september/christian-decline-inexorable-nones-rise-pew-study.html.

Sisters of the Road. "Mission and Philosophies." https://www.sistersoftheroad.org/mission-and-philosophy.

Smither, Edward L. *Mission as Hospitality: Imitating the Hospitable God in Mission.* Eugene, OR: Wipf & Stock, 2021.

Snyder, Susanna. *Asylum-Seeking, Migration and Church: Exploration in Practical, Pastoral, and Empirical Theology*. New York: Routledge, 2016.

Soerens, Matthew, et al. *Welcoming the Stranger: Justice, Compassion and Truth in the Immigration Debate.* Downer's Grove, IL: InterVarsity, 2018.

Soto, Ariel G. Ruiz. "Record Breaking Migrant Encounters at the U.S.-Mexico Border Overlook the Bigger Story." October 2022. https://www.migrationpolicy.org/news/2022-record-migrant-encounters-us-mexico-border.

Southern Poverty Law Center and the National Holocaust Museum. "A History: Asylum in the United States." October 2, 2018. https://www.splcenter.org/20181002/history-asylum-united-states.

Spivey, Robert A., et al. "Mark: The Gospel of Suffering." In *Anatomy of the New Testament,* edited by Robert A. Spivey et al., 51–75. Minneapolis: Augsburg Fortress, 2013.

Sri, Edward. "Mercy Melts 'Hidden Sin.'" *Stay Catholic.* https://staycatholic.com/part-7-mercy-melts-hidden-sin/.

St. Johns, Newfoundland. "A New Wave of Mass Migration Has Begun." *The Economist,* May 28, 2023. https://www.economist.com/finance-and-economics/2023/05/28/a-new-wave-of-mass-migration-has-begun.

Stanford Encyclopedia of Philosophy. "Simone Weil." November 24, 2021. https://plato.stanford.edu/entries/simone-weil/#.

Statista. "Number of Refugee Admissions in the U.S. from the Fiscal Year of 1990 to the Fiscal Year of 2022." https://www.statista.com/statistics/200061/number-of-refugees-arriving-in-the-us/#statisticContainer.

St. Clair, Raquel A. "Perspectives on Discipleship and Suffering in Mark." In *Call and Consequences: A Womanist Reading of Mark*, 39–56. Minneapolis: Augsburg Fortress, 2008.

Stevens, Marty E. *Leadership Roles of the Old Testament: King, Prophet, Priest and Sage.* Eugene, OR: Cascade, 2012.

Sufrin, Julia. "3 Things to Know: Cultural Humility." Hogg Blog, November 5, 2019. https://hogg.utexas.edu/3-things-to-know-cultural-humility.

Sunshine, Glenn. "The Church's Response to Pandemics Throughout History and the Lessons for Today." *Missions in the Age of Coronavirus* (July 1, 2020). https://www.missionfrontiers.org/issue/article/the-churchs-response-to-pandemics-throughout-history-and-the-lessons-for-to#.

Swenson, Kristen M. *Living Through Pain: Psalms and the Search for Wholeness.* Waco, TX: Baylor University Press, 2005.

Syracuse University TRAC Immigration. "A Sober Assessment of the Growing U.S. Asylum Backlog." December 22, 2022. https://trac.syr.edu/reports/705/.

Tennies, Tyler R. "Book Review: Fault Lines: The Social Justice Movement and Evangelical's Looming Catastrophe." *Liberty University Journal of Statesmanship and Public Policy* 2 (2021) 1–6. https://digitalcommons.liberty.edu/cgi/viewcontent.cgi?article=1119&context=jspp.

Thornton, Ed. "What Causes People to Lose Their Faith?" *Church Times*, March 1, 2019. https://www.churchtimes.co.uk/articles/2019/1-march/features/features/what-causes-people-to-lose-their-faith.

Thurman, Howard. *Jesus and the Disinherited.* Boston: Beacon, 1949.

Turner, Daniel. *Charity the Bond of Perfection. A Sermon, the Substance of Which Was Preached at Oxford, November 16, 1780. On Occasion of the Re-establishment of a Christian Church of Protestant Dissenters in That City: With a Brief Account of the State of the Society.* Oxford: J. Buckland; J. Johnson; E. and C. Dilly, 1780.

Tobon, Monica. "The Normativity of Measure in Gregory Nazianzus' and Gregory of Nyssa's Orations on Love for the Destitute Poor." *Vox Patrum 78* (2021) 242.

TRAC Immigration. "Record Number of Asylum Cases in FY 2019." January 8, 2020. https://tracreports.org/immigration/reports/588/.

Tucker, Dennis. "Old Testament Through the Lens of Migration." Presentation to DaySpring Baptist Church (October 21, 2021).

United Nations. "World Migration Report (2022)." https://worldmigrationreport.iom.int/world-migration-report-2022-key-findings.

United Nations High Commission for Refugees. "UNHCR's Views on Asylum Claims from Individuals Fleeing Violence by Gangs and Other Organized Criminal Groups in Central America and Mexico." September 2022. https://www.unhcr.org/en-us/631f424f4.pdf.

USA Facts. "How Many People Seek Asylum in the US?" July 13, 2023. https://usafacts.org/articles/how-many-people-seek-asylum-in-the-us/.

U.S. Citizenship and Immigration Services. "Obtaining Asylum in the United States." May 31, 2022. https://www.uscis.gov/humanitarian/refugees-and-asylum/asylum/obtaining-asylum-in-the-united-states.

U.S. Health and Human Services. "New Surgeon General Advisory Raises Alarm about the Devastating Impact of the Epidemic of Loneliness and Isolation in the United States." May 3, 2023. https://www.hhs.gov/about/news/2023/05/03/new-surgeon-general-advisory-raises-alarm-about-devastating-impact-epidemic-loneliness-isolation-united-states.html.

Villegas, Alexander, and Frances Robles. "Conflicts Over Indigenous Land Become More Violent in Central America." *New York Times* (March 9, 2020). https://www.nytimes.com/2020/03/09/world/americas/central-america-indigenous-conflicts.html.

Villegas, Isaac S. "A Liturgy in the Borderlands." *The Christian Century*, October 4, 2022. https://www.christiancentury.org/article/features/liturgy-borderlands.

———. "Providing Sanctuary as Witness: Standing in Solidarity with Immigrants." https://www.youtube.com/watch?v=mL53HzmQSis.

Wehner, Peter. "The Evangelical Church Is Breaking Apart: Christians Must Reclaim Jesus from His Church." *The Atlantic*, October 24, 2021. https://www.theatlantic.com/ideas/archive/2021/10/evangelical-trump-christians-politics/620469/.

Wells, Sam. "Being With." St. Martin-in-the-Fields. August 2, 2019. https://www.youtube.com/watch?v=w2Zci7KBXms.

———. "'Being With' by Revd Dr Sam Wells." Diocese of Oxford. https://www.youtube.com/watch?v=xpycHbCcuXs.

West, John Lee, et al. *Emotional Intelligence for Religious Leaders*. Lanham, MD: Rowman & Littlefield, 2018.

Westchester University. "Tuckman's Stages of Group Development." https://www.wcupa.edu/coral/tuckmanStagesGroupDelvelopment.aspx#.

Williams, Thaddeus J. "Putting First Things First: The Gospel and Social Justice in that Order." *Journal of Christian Legal Thought* 8 (2018). https://www.christianlegalsociety.org/sites/default/files/2019-04/CLSJournal_Winter2019_web.pdf.

Willimon, William. *Leading With the Sermon*. Minneapolis: Fortress, 2020.

Winckles, Andrew O., and Angela Rehbein, eds. *Women's Literary Networks and Romanticism: "A Tribe of Authoresses."* Liverpool: Liverpool University Press, 2018.

Wright, Tom. *Luke for Everyone*. Louisville, KY: Westminster John Knox, 2004.

www.ingramcontent.com/pod-product-compliance
Lightning Source LLC
LaVergne TN
LVHW090525110826
845146LV00003B/980

* 9 7 9 8 3 8 5 2 5 6 1 7 4 *